BOLDER
NOT OLDER

NICKY HAMBLETON-JONES

Synergy Publishing
Newberry, FL 32669
publishwithsynergy.com

Bolder Not Older
By Nicky Hambleton-Jones

Copyright© 2025 by Nicky Hambleton-Jones

All Rights reserved. Under International Copyright Law, no part of this publication may be reproduced, stored, or transmitted by any means–electronic, mechanical, photographic (photocopy), recording, or otherwise–without written permission from the publisher and copyright holder.

Printed in the United Kingdom.

International Standard Book Number: ISBN 978-1-61036-911-4

Interior Layout and Cover Design:
Cris Convery

Photography:
Kieron Webb

BOLDER
NOT OLDER

NICKY HAMBLETON-JONES

Synergy
PUBLISHING

CONTENTS

Introduction – New Beginnings　　　　　　　　　　　　3

Week 1 – How to be Bold　　　　　　　　　　　　　　19

Week 2 – Chronicles of Your Wardrobe　　　　　　　35

Week 3 – Style Your Mind　　　　　　　　　　　　　47

Week 4 – Foundations of a Flawless Fit　　　　　　　57

Week 5 – Apples and Pears, Who Actually Cares　　　71

Week 6 – The Great Closet Cleanout　　　　　　　　89

Week 7 – The Wardrobe Edit　　　　　　　　　　　117

Week 8 – All Things Bold & Bright　　　　　　　　133

Week 9 – The Print Effect　　　　　　　　　　　　151

Week 10 – Bling It On　　　　　　　　　　　　　　167

Week 11 – Anatomy of an Outfit　　　　　　　　　183

Week 12 – Mastering the Shopping Game　　　　　197

Conclusion – A Bold Invitation　　　　　　　　　　215

> *"It's time to turn Oldness into Boldness."*

INTRODUCTION

NEW BEGINNINGS

Hello beautiful,

I am so happy we've found each other. I'm going to take you on a rip-roaring ride that's going to leave you utterly transformed, head to toe. Twelve weeks from now you are going to be different; bolder, braver and a stand-out individual. Oh yes! I'm so excited for you. I can already see how much potential you have to look and feel amazing, even if you can't quite see it or feel it for yourself yet. But you will, you'll see. All you have to do is follow the process I've set out for you, right here in this book and watch the magic unfold.

And no, it's not going to be hard work, in fact it's going to feel great. You know why? Because you really want this. You're sick and tired of feeling undesirable and lacklustre. I hear you. It's not a great place to be, especially when you look ahead and all you can see is oldness. From now on we're going to turn oldness into boldness. Yes, you are going to learn how to unleash your true style identity, so your age becomes nothing more than a number and you feel like you can still conquer the world.

I am going to take your hand and walk you step by step through my tried and tested transformation process that I use whenever I style my clients. When I look at you, all I see is the amazing potential you have to look and feel incredible. I don't care what size you are, how big your tummy or thighs are, how tall or short you are… that's all just noise.

Think of this as your secret, the key to unlocking your inner goddess, the style maven hidden and suppressed inside, long forgotten but still very much there. Together we are going to dig her out.

You're going to meet her soon and when you do she's going to become your NBF (new best friend) for life. The best part is, she'll never go away or let you down because she is YOU, the version of yourself that you've never tapped into, or simply forgotten about. She'll be there every time you look in the mirror, when you take that bold step and push yourself out of your comfort zone, when you fall and think you're defeated. She will be there to remind you of your strength and your resilience. It's honestly the most powerful feeling in the world, knowing that you're not alone. Your alter ego will stand with you no matter what, enabling you to hold your head high and put your best foot (and outfit) forward, no matter what. I'm going to show you how to create and leverage her.

Your style directive

When I sat down to write this book I felt totally overwhelmed with the amount of information I wanted to include. There are so many things, tips that I know that can help you to achieve style perfection, that I didn't want to leave anything out. Then I realised this isn't a book about do's and don'ts; it's not about achieving style perfection, as in fact there is no such thing, what's perfect for one person will be someone else's worst nightmare. The main purpose of this book is to open your eyes and inspire your creativity to experiment and have fun with fashion. To develop the desire to look and feel good everyday and not just throw on something for the sake of it. To be more adventurous with your outfits and the clothes you wear, I want you to unleash your style queen. If I can help you to do that on even the smallest level, then this book will have achieved what I set out to do; to be Bolder not Older, to not be held back or limited by your age in terms of the clothing choices we make. If I can help each and every person that reads this book to achieve that, then it really doesn't matter whether I've covered every detail, it will have been enough.

Why you are here

This book is for you if:

- **You feel trapped in your wardrobe.**

- **You second guess everything you wear based on what other people think.**

- **You feel, how do I say it….blah. Off kilter, wondering if this is it from now on?**

- **You've become invisible, no wolf whistles, no compliments, in fact you've forgotten what it even feels like to enjoy being the centre of attention. You're happy just being there, settling in the corner, the person everyone relies on, but no one really takes notice of your presence.**

I hear you, as my mum used to say…"getting older isn't for the faint hearted". But it doesn't have to be that way, you can choose to be bolder or older. It's up to you, not society, what you become.

"You can choose to be bolder or older. It's up to you, not society, what you become."

INTRODUCTION

Why I wrote this book.

There have been many times in my life as I look back on the ebb and flow of my success that I wondered why I hadn't been a lawyer or an accountant. It might seem ridiculous, but if I'm honest, my career so far has resembled a hair raising rollercoaster ride. There have been a few highs and a lot of lows.

"Yes. I lost everything."

From an outside perspective people just see the fact that I've been on national TV as the ultimate achievement, but few know of the sacrifices and challenges I faced to get there and of the total and instant implosion of everything I'd worked so hard to achieve, when I was dropped. Yes. I lost everything, well not everything, just my TV career. This may not seem like a big deal, but when you're ambitious and you strive for success, to lose it all at the point when big things were just coming to fruition, was a massive blow.

Coupled with the relentless bullying, trolling and abuse I received from the media, to say my confidence was rock bottom would be an understatement. There would be days when I would sit on the side of my bed, tears streaming down my face, retching. I felt so sick at the thought of having to face the world and act as if nothing had happened. I suffered in silence, I painted a picture where I had chosen this path and was happy with the outcome when in reality I was broken. The things that saved me were clothes and Ava (I'll tell you more about her later in the book). I told myself that no matter how bad I felt, all I had to do was get out of bed, get dressed and put my red lippy on. I did this day after day, whether I had anything in the diary or not. Week after week, I showed up every day, dressed for the career I desperately wanted to get back, my red lippy firmly in place. Slowly, and I mean very slowly, I started to feel better. I told myself that as long as I liked what I saw in the mirror I would be ok, and I honestly believe that's true.

It's been 16 years since that fateful day and I've never stopped trying to be the best version of myself. You see, you can kick someone down the hill but when they stand up and look brighter, fitter and stronger than they did before, it's the one thing that they can't take away from you. No matter how much you may feel like a failure, you don't have to look like one! What you wear is such a powerful tool, and so closely connected with your self worth, it deserves more than just a throw on in the morning. What you wear is such a powerful tool, and so closely connected with your self worth, it deserves more than just a throw on in the morning.

So if you're feeling flat, perhaps you've had some life knocks too, you've got older and feel like you've lost your edge, know this, I am exactly like you and if I can still hold my head up high and own my own catwalk, so can you.

I wrote this book to show you how to put your best self forward, no matter what your age, size or shape, they're only numbers. What you bring to the table is soul, and a whole lot of life experience, you're just lacking a bit of spice But there is a bolder version inside of you and it's time to dig her out baby!

BOLDER NOT OLDER

What this book is about

This is a book predominantly about how to transform your style, but it goes a lot deeper than that. Getting dressed every day is something we all have to do, bit like brushing teeth. So you'd think that because you have to do something on a daily basis we would all be masters at it, but think about it, so few dress really well. Why? Being able to curate a fabulous outfit and carry it off in style requires courage, confidence, and self-belief. Yes, a great outfit will give you a huge confidence boost, but it's only when you consistently turn up, and invest in improving the way you dress each day that long-lasting change happens. That's when you really transition from boring to bold, average to amazing. This book is a style guide with a difference. Over the next 12 weeks you're going to work on your mindset and your wardrobe; internal and external change, as one goes hand in hand with the other. I've seen it so many times where I transform someone on the outside, but they haven't embraced it on the inside and guess what, within a few weeks they're back to where they were. You have to REALLY want to be Bolder and *live* a Bolder life for this process to work. Unless you have the desire, nothing is going to happen. So, my question for you is, how badly do you want to be Bolder not Older? If it's a lot, then you, my gorgeous friend, are in the right place. Let's get to work.

Creating your alter ego

Let me start by introducing you to Ava, Ava Storm. Ava's my alter ego. I may sound a bit weird, but let's face it we don't all wake up feeling like we can conquer the world each and every day, especially as we get older. Sometimes we simply need an extra helping hand and that's where Ava comes in. She's the perfect embodiment of everything I want to be. Super confident, focused and unwavering on her mission. Whenever I need an extra big dose of confidence and self belief, perhaps I've got a press engagement or important meeting when I need to be on top form, I channel Ava Storm.

Let me tell you a little about Ava and you'll see why she's such a powerful tool to leverage.

Ava is:

Confident and Charismatic

Ava exudes self-assurance in every situation. Her confidence is magnetic, and people are drawn to her presence.

Fiercely Independent

Ava is not someone who depends on others for validation or support. She stands on her own, forging her path with determination and resilience.

BOLDER NOT OLDER

Meet Ava

Bold and Daring

Ava is unafraid of challenges and faces them head-on. She takes the lead and enjoys testing her limits.

Elegant and Stylish

While bold, She blends sophistication with an edge—perhaps dressed in sleek, sharp lines, with a touch of drama.

Who wouldn't want to be like Ava right? Whenever I'm struggling to pluck up the confidence to take action to do something, I just ask myself 'What would Ava do?' Yip, you can picture the scene, less than 5 seconds and I'm on it! She is the force of nature I want to be like. Super human and totally unrealistic but when you're trying to do big things you need to step out of who you currently are and believe that you can be anything you want to be.

An alter ego allows you to circumvent those limiting beliefs about yourself, because you're not being yourself. Instead you're being someone with positive beliefs, about the world and yourself. For example when I have to do something that scares the hell out of me, I stand in front of the mirror and repeat one of Ava's mantras (also invented by me) to myself… 'I fear nothing, and face everything'. It's a really powerful force for you to lean on and tap into as you go through this process and stumble into moments of doubt. Because you will.

Transformation is change and with change comes resistance, a disruption of the status quo, an imbalance of the natural equilibrium of the life you've carefully garnered and created. As you start to stir up your routine and change your thinking along with your outfits, there will naturally be a pull to go back to the way things were.

That place was easy and comfortable, but it was also the reason you picked up this book in the first place. Tapping into your alter ego when you feel resistant to change, (those voices in your head that pop and tell you how ridiculous you are, you know the ones I mean), will help remind you of why you're here and where you're going. It's a really powerful tool, one that many successful people use. Think of your alter ego as your silent weapon, only you will know about her and who she is.

For many years I've transformed men and women, so I'm very aware of the emotional rollercoaster people embark on to get to where they want to be. Changing one's outward appearance may seem superficial, but to truly transform yourself, you have to change the way you perceive yourself and that takes time, dedication and practice. In the moments when you falter, your alter ego can really help you to 'keep your heels on' and not give up on the process.

I find having Ava by my side when I need her a very powerful tool. She makes me feel invincible, like I can achieve anything. Especially useful on days when you feel the rejection of the world on your shoulders and just getting out of bed is an effort. For Ava it's never an effort. A quick switch to her, and I'm off.

Before you start this 12-week transformation process, I'd encourage you to spend time creating your alter ego, if you don't have one already. It's a really fun thing to do, a bit like creating your very own superhero.

Start by thinking of a name for them, and then break down their traits using the following headlines. You don't have to go into as much detail, but I think doing so helps you to really embody who she is, so that when you need her, you know exactly what you're getting.

Appearance

What does she look like? Ava Storm has jet black long hair and piercing blue eyes; in fact she's very like Susie Glass in *The Gentleman*. Her style is a blend of edgy and sophisticated, she loves sleek tailoring with an element of sexy in rich jewel tones that contrast with her hair and pale skin.

Personality

What are her personality traits? Think of this as the traits you wish you had and throw them all into your alter ego, that way when you step into her, you become her. Ava Storm is confident, intelligent, independent and resilient. It's worth embellishing each trait in more detail, the more specific you are the more powerful she will be.

Skills and Talents

What does she do well? Again, think of your alter ego as having complementary skills and talents to yours. If you find standing at the front of a room giving a talk, hard, then your alter ego will be a brilliant keynote speaker. She will relish speaking engagements and inspiring an audience with her words. See how powerful that is? Immediately you feel more confident as you step into new shoes and embody powerful characteristics, even though it's all in your head, our brain is a very powerful tool.

Style Challenge 1

> Create an alter ego. Make her as bold as you can, as they will inspire and motivate you to make bolder choices too. Write down their features and traits and keep them next to your bed, that way you can keep reminding yourself of who they are, until it becomes second nature.

You're going to need this new friend over the following 12 weeks and beyond. She will ensure you stay on the path and don't fall back into your old ways.

Right, enough chat, diary out, pen at the ready and dates booked. Your 12-week programme starts tomorrow, or as soon as you're ready. Let's do this. See you, (and your alter ego) in Week 1.

Let us begin

Are you ready, my style queen? If yes, tomorrow we start, but today I want you to get out your diary and carve out at least 3–4 hours a week over the next 12 weeks to work on your transformation. Some chapters will take longer than others to complete. The wardrobe and shopping chapters in particular will take more time to do well. Don't stress if you fall behind with some of the tasks. Just stick to the process and keep doing the exercises as and when you're able to, just don't give up on the book. If you're dedicated you can definitely complete it in 12 weeks, but if it takes a month more, that's fine. How long the process takes, doesn't matter, as long as your desire and commitment is there. That being said, don't worry, you don't have to wait till the end for your transformation to be revealed. There's no final mirror moment here as your transformation in fact begins right now, and as each week unfolds you will visibly start to change one week at a time.

Small changes = big differences so dedicate some time to the programme. It really does help to schedule the time to work on this process in your diary, as that way you're setting aside time to invest in yourself and are more likely to stick to it. To be on the safe side, block out half a day a week, which you can allocate as one session or spread across a few days. Perhaps you're a morning person in which case getting up half an hour earlier will work best for you, if you're an evening thinker, book a date with yourself a few times a week or carve out a morning or afternoon at the weekend. This isn't meant to be a chore, design it around your schedule, commitments, whatever works best for you. Be realistic and create a plan you're more likely to stick to rather than one that causes you to crash and burn after a few weeks and throw the book out the window; please don't do that. Think of it as going to the gym 3 times a week, you have to book out the time in your calendar to do it, this is no different.

Invest in a journal

An A4 empty workbook that looks gorgeous, and you can write in. You'll also need a fabulous pen to write with. (I'll explain more about this soon).

I recommend you read a chapter at the start of the week or the weekend before, so you know what the style challenges I've set out for each week are. These are clearly marked in each chapter. Some weeks there are more challenges than others but it will give you an idea of what's ahead so you can plan accordingly, and even block out a bit more time if you need to. But just to reiterate again, if you run over by a few days or miss a week, that's ok. Just stick to the process, and if it helps, make yourself a chart and cross off each week as you complete it so you have a visual sense of where you are and can celebrate how far you've come along the way. Great style is a journey not a flash in the pan. Well done for getting to the start line, I'll be your expert driver for the journey, we're going to have so much fun.

> "Great style is a journey not a flash in the pan."

INTRODUCTION

HOW TO BE BOLD

And here we go…

Goodbye old life, hello to your new bolder self. I hope you had a lot of fun creating your alter ego, keep her close by your side and feel free to introduce yourself to her in the mirror. Get to know her, the better you know her the easier it is to become her when you need to. Your alter ego will enable you to rise to the challenge in high stakes moments.

Let's face it, choosing to be bolder won't be easy, if it was, everyone would do it. There is no comfort zone, no stretchy leggings and sweatshirt to wrap yourself in. Oh no, it's about raising your game, wearing your best outfit, stepping out and claiming who you are each and every day. Phew, does that feel overwhelming? It probably does a bit right now, and that's ok. Don't fight it, just sit with it and whatever you do don't run away as crossing that finish line will be so worth it, especially when you do it with style.

Being 'bolder' is having the courage to wear something different, something that stands out (for all the right reasons). It's accepting that where you're at is a little meh and you want something more. You're fed up with being invisible, hiding your true colours.

It's time.

Welcome to Week 1 on your transformation journey.

Let's go!

What does it mean to be Bold?

Bold (Bold-er, Bold-est)

adjective

- **(of a person, action, or idea) showing a willingness to take risks; confident and courageous.**
- **(of a colour, design, or shape) having a strong, vivid, or clear appearance.**

"Being 'bolder' is having the courage to wear something different, something that stands out."

The mid-life invisibility cloak

Invisible Women Syndrome is a real phenomenon. According to a survey done by Gransnet that studied 2,000 women, 70% of women believe they become "invisible" as they get older, starting at around age 50.

Many women reported that the moment they turned 50, people stopped seeing them. People push past them in queues, and men look through them.

One thing I hear my clients say a lot, is 'I feel invisible'. 'No one notices me anymore', which is then caveated with 'oh well I guess that's just what happens when you get older?!'

No, it is not. Such a syndrome does not have to be your fate. You get to decide your place in this world – not anyone else.

The reason you feel invisible is because YOU have subconsciously chosen to make yourself invisible. It's got nothing to do with the world and everything to do with you. Take a moment to reflect over the past 20 years of your life. Do you still put the same amount of effort into the way you dress? Do you bother with make-up? Is your wardrobe vibrant and colourful or toned down to reflect a more mature version of yourself?

"Style has the power to bring visibility to the often unseen."

Whether it's conscious or not, so many women naturally tone down their appearance as they get older. Why? Lots of reasons: body shape changes, time and budget limitations, preconceived ideas about what you can and can't wear past a certain age; mutton dressed as lamb connotations. Where do these preconceptions come from? Mostly from ourselves, and also from our friends and society at large. We are inherently followers, even more so as we get older and social media certainly doesn't help. If we surround ourselves with people who have chosen to mute their appearance, for whatever reason, chances are you will too. It takes a lot of courage to be a trail blazer and set your style apart from the pack, particularly the older you get.

Fitting in is easy, low stress, low maintenance; standing out takes a lot of confidence and self-belief but the payoff is huge. One's appearance often feels like such a small cog in the wheel of life, but when you get it right and you feel good in what you wear, you discover renewed energy to tackle the other areas of your life that also need attention. It's that powerful.

Unashamedly you

Many women, and I think particularly in the UK, feel embarrassed about investing in their appearance, for fear of being called vain, superficial, conceited. None of which are flattering, and I totally get why you'd do anything to avoid being called one of those terms. But here's the thing, people who are content and happy with where they are in life will never refer to someone else who's taking pride in their appearance as vain. They will instead shower them with compliments and positive affirmations. On the other hand, the opposite is true for those that are less happy with their appearance and that's nothing to do with you and everything to do with them. There is nothing wrong with taking pride in the way you look, in fact, it should be mandatory. You have one life to live, take care of what you have and make the most of your assets. That's self-respect not vanity.

There is an interesting dichotomy between northern European and southern European women. In the north, women are embarrassed to admit needing or craving 'me time' to focus on themselves, their health, looks etc. There is this puritan perception of our value – we need to make everything perfect for everyone else, and if we happen to be gorgeous great, but we shouldn't waste time working at it (it's considered vain if we do). Southern European women embrace these things without that unnecessary shame. Why wouldn't you do everything you can to be fabulous? Brene Brown famously said "Shame corrodes the very part of us that believes we are capable of change".

So, if your instinctive reaction to investing in your appearance and looking good is, 'what will everyone else think?' 'Will I be judged?' Then look to surround yourself with people who are comfortable with looking and feeling good every day. Women who embrace their inner princess with humour and kindness – rather than seeing it as a negative.

It goes without saying that you uplevel your appearance to the environment you spend most of your time in. If everyone around you is constantly in sweatpants and hoodies, you will most likely be too. Find a new tribe, use their energy to motivate yourself and feel comfortable with stepping into your power or block out the noise in your head that's screaming, you're too old, too fat, too whatever to embark on this transformation journey. You can do this and do it well. You deserve to look and feel amazing, no matter what.

Feeling invisible is unpleasant but it's also a choice. You can choose to be seen or you can choose to fade into the background. Either option is equally valid. Some people are very happy to wait on the sidelines while others want to shout their presence from the rooftops.

The fact that you're reading this book tells me you aren't ready to put your feet up and let it all go – you want to be seen, to feel alive, to embrace fear and do it anyway. This is the moment where you must choose to be seen. If you choose yes, then I will help you achieve that dream.

> **"Feeling invisible is unpleasant but it's also a choice. You can choose to be seen or you can choose to fade into the background."**

BOLDER NOT OLDER

Get your legs out girl!

Wear the damn shorts!

A slogan made famous by fitness giant Sweaty Betty, #wearthedamnshorts. It resonated with me as I too was held back by preconceptions of myself and what other people would think. I've never had naturally great legs, so I shied away from wearing shorts completely, opting instead for cropped trousers. Then I turned 50 and thought, what would Ava do and the answer was loud and clear – get your legs out girl! So, I tried on a pair of short denim shorts and the rest is history. Now I wear shorts all summer long and I've never felt more empowered every time I do, thank you Ava! It doesn't matter how old you are or what society says you should or shouldn't be wearing, if you want to wear something – just do it!

Going back to that survey by Gransnet, 65% of women believe that style and confidence have more to do with how people are treated than age. That my friend is why you are here. If you want to stop feeling invisible, like a casual observer of your own life, then investing in your appearance will 100% improve how people treat you and most importantly how you feel about yourself.

The lady on the bus

Betty Klimenko is most known as being the heiress to the Westfield empire and the first female owner of a motorsport team in Australia. But in other circles, she's known as the lady on the bus in the tutu. "Too many women tend to get into a place where they wake up and do the same thing all day. They never do anything to spark their life, to make them enjoy every moment… and then they turn around and they go, 'when did I become so old?' You don't become anything… you allow. You allow yourself to become old." Betty simply refuses to become an old lady… which for her means allowing herself to stay silly, to stay playful, and to wear whatever the hell you feel like wearing, in her case a tutu on the bus. Love it.

> "You don't become old; you allow yourself to get old."

Be the queen of your style

If there was ever a lady who was the epitome of 'Bold' it was Queen Elizabeth II. Throughout her 70-year reign, not once did she allow her style to falter. Always immaculately turned out, in a vibrant colour head-to-toe with accessories to complement. She didn't worry what other people thought, she dressed for herself, with her main intention being to stand out in a crowd and be visible, which she always did.

Wallpaper the ceiling

When a woman turns 50 there are usually two responses, take your foot off the pedal or apply extra pressure. There is this mindset that if you haven't achieved all your goals by 50 then you've missed the boat and it's unlikely to happen. Age 50 is a line that we subconsciously draw in the sand separating our youth from our older years. With that comes an instant mental shutdown of what we can and can't still achieve. But there are so many inspiring women who defy that line and really come into their own and achieve huge success in their later years.

- Ruth Bader Ginsberg was a Supreme Court Judge in the US until she was 87.
- Hillary Clinton was 68 when she ran for the US Presidency.
- Maye Musk became the oldest woman to grace the cover of Sports Illustrated at 74.
- Arianna Huffington started The Huffington Post at 54.
- Louise Hay launched Hay House publishing at 62; one of the largest non-fiction publishing companies in the world.
- Gladys Burrill ran her first marathon in 2004 at the age of 86.
- Iris Apfel became a model at 97.

And that's just a handful of women I know about, I know there are loads more who are slaying the world after 50 and beyond. All these women demonstrate that age is a number that doesn't dictate or define your success potential, that's totally down to you. I personally have a lot I still want to achieve in my lifetime, so I hope I'll be able to add my name to that list one day. And you? How old will you be when you smash your biggest goal yet?

Here's the thing, ladies. Visibility has everything to do with your mindset, style, and surroundings and absolutely nothing to do with your age. Positive, vibrant women are never invisible, no matter what the birth date on their driver's licence says. So wallpaper that ceiling so it no longer feels like an end but something wildly creative and exciting to look up to.

Self-perception and self-talk

What we believe about ourselves is critical. Sitting around moaning about our weight, age spots, creaky knees, and hot flushes are fine so long as we are balancing those messages with something positive. The way we speak to ourselves – and about ourselves – matters. Why? Because those messages sink in.

If you spend a week telling yourself you are old, ugly, and undesirable, guess what? At the end of that week, you're going to feel old, ugly, and undesirable. Furthermore, your behaviour will reinforce this. Your posture, your tone of voice, and your choices will align with that self-perception.

And guess what? People respond accordingly.

So what can you do?

You can't control other people, but you can control the way you show up in the world. You can fill yourself with so much strength, encouragement, and daring that suddenly, what's happening outside of you matters a bit less. This is where Ava has played a big part in helping me to reprogramme my negative talk to a more positive force and where your alter ego can be a powerhouse for you too.

Small positive habits can make a big difference to how you respond to life's calamities. No one can take you down unless you allow them too. Always putting your best face forward helps you to feel like you're winning, even if you're not, which is half the battle won. Having Ava Storm in my handbag helps too.

> "You can fill yourself with so much strength, encouragement, and daring that suddenly, what's happening outside of you matters a bit less."

How to be bolder

Here are my top tips for living a bolder life

Don't go out without lipstick... ever

It may sound silly, but lipstick is one of those things that people only wear when they've made an effort with their outfit or are going somewhere special. By making a point of always wearing lipstick you are subconsciously sending a message to your brain that today is a special day. That in turn will trigger an intention to dress better, which will immediately result in a more confident outlook. Trust me it works. Like you, I've had many setbacks over my life, some big enough to knock the wind out of my sails and leave me clutching straws. But each time I get knocked, I tell myself, all I have to do is get up, get dressed, put my lippy on and go to the gym. Yes, I have no issues with wearing lipstick to the gym, it's just how I roll and you know what, it works!

For the purposes of this 12 week exercise, I'd like you to wear your lipstick more often, but also to be bolder with your lipstick colour choices too. If you tend to favour neutral tones, pop into your nearest make-up counter and ask for advice on which brighter shades would suit you best. My advice is to do this every day for the duration of this 12-week programme and see how you feel. You may feel overdressed on day 1, but by day 50 you won't even notice you're doing it. It will just become part of who you are. Trust me when I say no one will bat an eyelid, but you will feel different, better, and that's all that matters.

Style Challenge 1

Make a point of wearing lipstick, the bolder the better, everywhere you go this week and keep reapplying throughout the day so it doesn't wear off.

Consider your tribe

Surround yourself with women who genuinely love themselves and who are living lives you respect and admire. Be mindful of who and what you allow in your world. That's not to say you should compare yourself to these women but use them more as a source of aspiration to give you the motivation and confidence to live a bolder life. Surround yourself with people who see you, hear you, respect you, and inspire you.

Recalibrate your socials

Change the people you follow on socials so the content in your feed aligns with how you want to look and live your life. Ensure you follow women that are up to a decade younger and at least a decade older than you. Take inspiration from younger and older women; where you've come from and where you are going. We all need inspiration from both ends of the spectrum. If we just focus on one direction, we can become depressed and closed minded.

Dress up

Vibrant, visible women dismiss those antiquated ideas of what is "age-appropriate" and I'm giving you permission to do this too. When you pull something you love out of your wardrobe, and it makes you feel fabulous: embrace it, own it and be visible in it. Wear what makes your heart scream. Style has so much more to do with confidence, than just what's in your wardrobe. It's more about your attitude than the clothes – it's about having no apologies for being a woman of a "certain age".

When you elevate your self-image, you elevate your life. You become – and stay – visible and I'm going to help you do just that. In this book I will show you how to create outfits that will make you feel seen for all the right reasons. So don't stress if you're thinking, I have nothing to wear. I am going to take you step by step through how to curate a wardrobe that makes you look and feel fabulous and most importantly, SEEN.

Make a choice

If you're the kind of woman who isn't ready to sit back and be old just yet – who wants to be seen, in surround sound, technicolor glory – there is one way to make sure that happens: choose to be seen. No one can stop you from showing up as your best, most empowered self at any age. What the world chooses to do with that is not your problem. Keep going, keep moving, keep dreaming, keep striving and most importantly get LOUD. If you really and truly want to be 'Bolder not Older' you need to purposefully strive to be the centrepiece at the table, the person that everyone notices. Yes YOU.

You can choose to be held back by your age or you can take more risks. You can stay in your comfort zone or push your boundaries. The key is to keep moving forward with grace, purpose and a big dose of style.

Paint the town...

It's simply impossible to live a bolder life without dressing in a more striking, vivid, bright, strong, eye-catching, conspicuous, and distinct manner. As much as a neutral outfit is elegant it's never going to uplevel your visibility stakes as much as wearing colour will. In this book, I will show you how to explore incorporating more colour into your daily outfits and how to style colour for true show-stopping impact. It may seem daunting, but as I said above, if you choose to be seen then painting the town red, or whatever colour you choose, is something you will soon become comfortable with.

Be active

For some of us this might be joining the gym, for others it's walking the dog or hiking outdoors. Choosing new adventures and going outside of your comfort zone helps to re-energise and boost confidence levels. Whatever you choose, it's important to stay active and mobile on a daily basis. Good posture, flexibility and high energy levels will enable you to continually take part in all the exciting things life has to offer. Each day is an adventure. Remember you are the conductor of your life...not the passenger!

> "...and you thought beauty was the outward show – but now you know the truth, my Love – it's always been the INNER FIRE..."
> **John Geddes.**

Glow

How many wrinkles you have is quite frankly irrelevant. True boldness comes from within. Wearing that lipstick, owning your style and taking part in as many of life's adventures as you're able to, will make your heart sing. When you feel happy, you will shine.

Being bolder is all about embracing life, your style and your outlook. Alter ego at the ready, this book will help you to uplevel your style which will in turn improve self esteem and boost your confidence to go live your life to the full. The fact that you're here means you've got this. Let the transformation begin.

What's important is starting each day with the mindset of putting on your best outfit, go OTT if you want to. Honestly, nobody cares, just do it and observe how liberating it feels. Start by taking risks with what you wear, no matter how uncomfortable it may feel. You're knocking down barriers, it might feel a bit awkward initially but soon, you won't even think about it. That's what we're aiming for.

Style Challenge 2

Make a point of dressing up each day this week. Don't worry about whether it looks good or not or whether you have clothes worthy of such a task, just do the best with what you've got; wear the clothes you've been saving for that special occasion.

Style Challenge 3

Take photos of each outfit you wear this week. In fact make a habit of doing this throughout this 12 week process. By the end it will give you a visual reminder of how far you've come as well as a catalogue of outfit combinations to refer to.

Enjoy it and I'll see you in Week 2.

WEEK 1

What you will need for next week:

- A journal
- A pen
- An A3 piece of cardboard or pin board
- Pins to stick things on your board
- Photos of your style through the decades

CHRONICLES OF YOUR WARDROBE

Welcome to Week 2

of your 12-week transformation programme. How did it feel wearing a bright lipstick and your best outfit each day last week? A bit uncomfortable at times hopefully. I say this because if you don't feel any resistance, you're not challenging yourself enough.

The universe loves keeping you in a safe status quo, the minute you try and do something different or daring, it will try to stop you and move you back to where you were, that's resistance. If you're not feeling it, you won't change. So embrace that feeling of discomfort, the more you feel it, embrace it and move through it the bigger your transformation will be.

You'll be relieved to hear that this week may be a bit easier, as we're going to focus on your past, the present and how you'd like to look in the future. Hopefully you've invested in a gorgeous journal and pen as you'll be needing them for this week's challenges, but I would encourage you to start journaling for 15 minutes every day as you go through this process and beyond. As mentioned previously, in order to really change the way you look and feel about yourself, you'll have to confront demons and emotions you didn't even know you had. You'll be reminded of issues you thought were dead and buried till they rear their ugly head again. Journaling will help you to process those feelings as they occur, so they don't build up and burst, the point where most people give up and walk away. I really want you to succeed as I can see your potential and I know if you stick with the programme you'll never look back.

Journaling is your safety net, the voice of reason when nothing makes sense, and you can't remember why you started this process in the first place. When my mother-in-law died, it happened so suddenly it was a shock. We were very close, she was my rock, my safe place when my world was in disarray. I just didn't know what to do with my grief. Life just moved on, kids had to be dropped at school, food prepared, laundry done and clients to style, there was no time or space to process how I felt. As a result, I just got more and more depressed, until a friend mentioned journaling. I ignored it at first, and then one day I picked up a pen and started to write and write and write. Within a few weeks I began to feel lighter and brighter, within a month I was back to my creative self. It was utterly transformative, and I still do it as often as I can, especially when I've got lots on my mind I need to let go of. It's a very powerful tool and one which will support you and have your back throughout this process if you use it.

Best way to start is today, now, make yourself a cup of tea, book out an hour in your work schedule and get comfortable. This is a week of two halves. First, we're going to look at the past, admire how far you've come and then we're going to focus on the future.

Your style journal

I'd like you to start your daily journaling practice, by writing down your story, I want to know everything about you. Where you've come from, where you're going and the bits in between. It doesn't matter what place you're currently in, it's how you got here that I'm interested in, as that's what makes you special. Whether it's a good journey or a troubled one, it's yours and you're the only one that's travelled this path. It's what makes you unique, special and real.

We live in a world of fakeness, everyone's airbrushing out their issues and only showing us their gloss. But when you get to your mid-life you realise everyone has the bad bits, no matter how perfect a persona someone puts out to the world, chances are they've had to kill a few demons to get there too.

So my point is, it's your journey that makes you Joan of Arc, that's the story you need to capture, that's what makes you a total warrior, a conqueror of all things. I want you to take all this energy you've put into surviving, getting through, keeping all the balls effortlessly in the air and put it into becoming a master of your own universe and no one else's. I wrote this book just for YOU. Because I know you deserve to look in that mirror, love what you see and go out and conquer the world. But in order for me to get you there, we need to take stock of where you are right now, how you got to where you are today, I want to know about the good times, the bad times and the bumps in the road. The triumphs, the losses and the boring bits in-between; the times when you were treading water for things to happen and the days when life in its essence couldn't have been better. When you felt on top of the world, what you were wearing and how you felt in that moment. I want you to write it all down, your life story so far; feel the pain at the sad bits and the joy when it all went right and the moments when you looked and felt your best.

It's in seeing how far you've come that you start to feel gratitude, pride and joy for just how amazing a human being you really are. This is an important step in your transformation journey; it's where you lay a strong foundation on which to build a better version of yourself. And you might rightly ask what this has to do about style? The answer is it's your identity, your uniqueness, the life scars and badges that make you, you.

Was there a time in your life when you took pride in what you wore? I need to know more? What were you wearing, doing and how did you dress?

For this task I'd like you to spend half an hour every morning, ideally first thing, and journal about yourself and your life. Laugh, cry and relive the moments where you truly felt alive, as that's the place we want to get you back to. What were you wearing, doing, who were you spending time with?

It's so easy to let one day blend into another, get up, get dressed, do the school run, go to work, make dinner, go to bed, repeat. Autumn, winter, spring, summer passing by....repeat. What felt like an eternity to reach 20 and the next thing you know, 40 is bearing down on you and then 50 too.

So let's start as we mean to go on together, embracing the past for the good that it's brought us and the lessons it's taught us and consider the elements that we'd like to recapture and put front and centre in your life again. Write as if you're telling me your life story through your fashion journey. We've just met and I've asked you where you're from.....go!

And remember you don't have to do this in one go, it's a daily practice, 30 minutes of journaling every morning or at a convenient time during the day about your story so far, the good, the bad and the wonderful.

Style Challenge 1

30 minutes of journaling every morning (or convenient time) to capture your life story. Write it like a novel if you want, you never know you may even publish it one day. Alternatively, if you simply pop it away in a drawer or destroy it afterwards, the process will be cathartic.

Style by design

For the second part of this week's task, we're going to do a deep dive into how you dress and by that I don't just mean right now I mean your story told through clothes. Let's have some fun and create a visual style board. Get yourself an A3 piece of cardboard or pinboard, rotate it horizontally and draw a line down the middle. On the LHS we're going to stick photos of your style through the years and on the RHS, pictures of the style we're aspiring to have.

This may seem a bit strange as I'm sure you're expecting me to just tell you what to wear, but if we're going to be successful, I need your full buy-in upfront. You have to feel excited about where you're headed. It's a collaborative process, me just telling you what you should and shouldn't do will go in one ear and out the other. Yes, you may adopt some of my advice, but it won't be enough to really change the way you dress and you'll quickly slip back into old habits and your comfy favourites. Which means the overall results won't be as powerful. But before we get to that, let's take stock of the here and now.

Fashion flashback

I'd like you to start off by digging out some old and I'm sure many shocking photos of a style past its sell by date. I'm talking about the cringy things we wore that we labelled cool. We've all been there. I went through a phase of wearing my dad's brown cardigan – I kid you not. Even I'm horrified at the thought, not just because I was wearing my dad's clothes but because it was brown, my least favourite colour now but back then it was cool. Honestly, what was I thinking? But despite what I think about it now, and trust me there are many more dubious fashion choices where that came from, that self-expression and experimentation with clothes forms a strong foundation for how one's style evolves. We all have to start somewhere. Once you've dug out those old photos however cringy they may be, stick them on the LHS of your board. Make sure to include photos from each decade of your life, the good, bad and the ugly. The photos that make you gasp, smile and cry with laughter. Focus especially on ones where you think 'wow, that was a great outfit', 'I looked really good then'…surprised because at the time you thought you were too fat or uncool and now looking back you're thinking, what was I worrying about? I'd give anything to look like that again. And that is exactly why we're bothering to go back down memory lane. To remind yourself that even in those moments when you actually looked good, you didn't think you were good enough. Isn't that crazy? Hey, I did it too. I wasn't born with a model figure and have had to work hard all my life to maintain a slim physique, but it never came close to the high standards of comparison I set for myself. Then a few years ago I was looking back at photos of myself with my then toddler, thinking and marvelling at how good I actually looked, when at the time I thought I wasn't good enough. Well, I can tell you right now, I have stopped doing that and you should too. It may have taken me 50 years to realise that however bad or imperfect you think you look at a point in time, chances are you'll look back and think you'd give anything to look like that again! I certainly did, and it got me thinking that a) never be too hard on yourself as nothing ever stays the same, time is always moving, and chances are the reason why you think you don't look great is actually nothing to do with you and everything to do with the high standards you've set for yourself. b) taking a trip down memory lane is a great reminder of the person you used to be, when you had fewer responsibilities maybe and your hormones weren't wreaking havoc with your mind and metabolism.

Admire your fashion choices and the effort you once put into your outfits, even if it's not your taste now, it's the thought and confidence you oozed in the clothes you wore, that we want to get you back to.

Nope, I hated it all.

And that may also be true. Not everyone has a fashion past they're proud of or even want to revisit again. Weight gain and body confidence issues may have limited your style choices from a young age. If this is you, then I'd still like you to journal about your story and stick a

WEEK 2

"Looking back at your style through the years is like flipping through a scrapbook of your evolving self—each outfit a snapshot of who you were, who you dared to be, and the journey of discovering your true essence."

42

few photos from your past as reminders of where you never want to go back to, but also include recent photos of the better version of you to remind you of your strength and resilience. If you can overcome those challenges, you are well equipped to get through this 12 week process with bells on.

Stop reading, make yourself a cup of tea and get started on the LHS of your style board. This may take a couple of days to get right, fine if it does. Spend an hour or so over a couple of days to get it finished. Once done, come back and read on.

Style Challenge 2

Create a style board.

Style forecast

Brilliant, well done. I hope that was a positive exercise whether you like the photos or not. Now for the really fun stuff, it's time to get started on the RHS of your board. This is the part where I want your creativity to really flow. I want you to go through Pinterest, the internet, Instagram, magazines and select photos of outfits and women who really inspire you by the way they dress. You'll notice that although this book is in essence a style guide, I have yet to talk about your body shape or what to wear. That's because right now, it's irrelevant. If I'm going to get you to the finish line, you

need to be on board. You need to have your eye on the prize, a vision of where you're heading as that's what's going to determine whether you get there or not. I can talk to you for the next 12 weeks about the best clothes to suit you and how to wear them but if you're not feeling inspired, excited about your potential to look and feel different, driven by a picture of what you're like to look like, it's just not going to happen. Even if it does, it won't last long and that's not why you're here. You're here because you want to look and feel different. You're in your mid-life and you're tired of feeling old, let's face it, you're bored with who you've become, and you want to have the confidence to make bolder choices so you can embrace looking and feeling your best no matter what your age.

Let me put this bluntly, I have no intention of ever ditching my heels or red lipstick. When I die, please make sure I'm wearing both as I want to go out continuing to wear them in heaven or wherever we all end up. You heard it here first. I want to continue feeling like me whatever my age. Yes, I'll have more wrinkles and my skin may not be as taught as it once was but none of those things need to stop me wearing what I love. In fact, it's all the more reason to keep doing so and if anything, uplevel the style stakes as the one benefit of ageing is you stop caring about what anyone else thinks – woohoo. If that's hard to imagine right now, by the end of this process you'll be living and breathing that mentality. If you don't like what I'm wearing, tough!

But I digress, let's get back to your vision board; developing a picture of how you'd like to look is such an important part of your transformation process, think of it as your guiding light. I want you to treat this exercise as if you have no limitations as to what you can wear; physically, financially, emotionally. Forget reality for a moment; the world is your oyster, if you had any shop or designer within your reach, what would you dream to wear, what styles do you love, what outfits would make you feel amazing? If you had your dream body shape, what would you wear and how would you wear it? Find pictures of people who inspire you by the outfits they choose. I'd also recommend you look for inspiration across all ages; someone older than you that makes really bold style choices could be the stimulus you never knew you needed.

Style board analysis

Prop your style board up in your study or somewhere you can look at it every day. Take 10 minutes to admire your efforts. It's so powerful to look at images that reinforce what you're aiming for. I have a vision board in my office filled with photos of things I want to achieve, places I want to go, outfits I'd love to wear. Mine is more of a life board, rather than style based, but either way, the reason a vision board is so powerful is because the brain assigns a higher 'value' to images than written words on a 'to-do' list. The more you look at those images, the more those goals are reinforced in your mind. Plus let's face it, style is a visual business, you can't write a nice outfit down on a to-do list, you have to see it in its entirety to be able to recreate it. The second reason a vision-style board is so powerful is it's a great motivator, it should get you excited to reach your destination. Don't worry about the 'how', we'll figure those bits out over the coming weeks, right now I just want you to stay with that feeling of excitement about achieving your desired look and reaching your transformation goal at the end of our 12 weeks together.

While you're admiring your efforts, I'd like you to write down in your journal any positives from the outfits you used to wear (LHS of your board). Anything you loved about your past style; key items that made you feel fabulous? Notice the colours you used to wear, have they changed over the years? Any observations there? I spent a large chunk of my teens dressed head to toe in black, part of my goth stage, yeah it wasn't great if I'm honest, probably why I'm drenched in colour now in an attempt to get over the darkness, ha ha!

We're not trying to recreate the past, rather use it more as an exercise of observation of how our style has evolved over the years. Noting any positives along the way that you may choose to recapture now, or not. No pressure either way. What we really want to focus on is the future.

Now look at the RHS of your board and write down any synergies between the outfits or items you've selected. Are they related to what you wear now or completely different? How big is the gap between where you are and where you want to be? There is no right or wrong way to do this. Just observe and write down anything that you notice in your journal.

Style Challenge 3

> Analyse your style board and journal about your discoveries.

That's it for this week. Not so bad was it? Hope you had a bit of a laugh along the way and feel inspired by the photos on your style board. Keep it in a prime location where you can see it everyday, at least until you've completed this process.

Keep looking at your board every day and we'll revisit it in more detail in Week 7.

Well done and see you next week.

STYLE YOUR MIND

Hello Week 3!

I hope you had a lot of fun digging out photo's of your past and adding lots of inspiring pictures, looks, people, and outfits that you'd love to wear to your style board. That's why I call it 'style by design', where you are completely free to wear anything, without limitations.

It's a bit like creating a mood board for a room you want to renovate, you start with all the inspo, colours, photo's and textures you'd love to incorporate and then narrow it down according to the room dimensions and budget constraints.

I really want to emphasise the word FREE here as, although you read it, I know you will instinctively still make choices based on what you think you can wear. Subconscious restrictions in your mind about your shape and situation (family, age, finances etc). We are so hard wired to be sensible and realistic, that letting our imaginations soar to places in our subconscious we've never tapped into can be hard. It's not something we do very often for fear that if we do, reality will probably be a disappointment, so best to be realistic. But if you don't do this, you'll never change at all. This is about allowing ourselves the freedom to explore new horizons without constraints.

Think of your brain as a large muscle. Over your life's journey you have trained it to think and respond in a certain way. It's like a well-trained dog, certain commands will always produce the same response as that's what you've trained your brain to do. Now I'm not a neurologist and I don't want to get too technical, but I do know that every thought or reaction we have is as a result of a neural pathway we've created, either through repetition or life experience. We have 1000's of neural pathways in our brains that are triggered every day in response to actions and thoughts that go through our minds. Changing the response and reaction to thoughts we have gets harder as we age and it's easy to get stuck in our comfort zones.

So, when I say choose anything you'd love to wear, you will instinctively choose things according to what you usually wear, what you think works and what you can afford, as that's how you've programmed your brain to respond. Our habits shape each day and our days ultimately make up the sum of our life. Therefore, what we do every day is a cardinal piece of our life's story and our overall well being. For many years, it was commonly believed that once we grew older, our brain could not change, similar to the adage "you can't teach an old dog new tricks". Now here's the interesting bit, no matter how old you are, you can still create new neural pathways in your brain by consistently changing your behaviours, habits and learning new skills, this is called neuroplasticity and that's where the real transformation happens as by learning new habits, you not only change your actions, you change the way you think at the same time.

It is important to practise repetition of the new activity as the pathway becomes stronger with the greater number of times the brain cells "fire" to conduct the new activity. The wiring together of brain cells makes the new behaviour feel routine and easier over time. It requires about 10,000 repetitions, translating to a minimum of three months of practice, to develop a new neural pathway and master a new pattern of behaviour.

Honey, you are what you are, live with it, embrace it and make the most of it.

Now you see why I've written this book as a 12-week programme. That's because it takes that long to permanently create new neural pathways in your brain. These new pathways will ensure you not only embed all the knowledge you've accumulated during this process, but also that you stick to it once the transformation process is complete. I don't want to bump into you a year down the line, only to discover your back where you started. I want this to be forever. I want you to feel bolder and not older from this point on.

Just as we can become frustrated with ourselves for repeating habits that are not helpful, we can free ourselves of those repetitions and practise new ones. How many times have we talked negatively to ourselves for overeating or not exercising? The key is to begin the new behaviour, repeat it many times, and associate it with as many positive thoughts, sensory experiences and visualisations as possible so that it becomes a new pathway of action and purpose in your brain.

So what has this got to do with style and the way you look?

The answer: a lot. When it comes to how we dress, mindset is everything. When we think about clothes and what we choose to wear, it's in essence an extension of who you think you are. The way you feel about yourself impacts the choices you make in your wardrobe. The negative voices in your head that stop you from embracing new styles. It's so much easier to stick with what's safe than face ridicule from family, friends or even strangers.

But as you start to embrace your true self and start to show up as the person you want to be (cue the style board work you've been doing) you will start to dress as if you're already that person, you begin to take ownership of this process and where you're heading. You start to believe that's who you really are. You're showing up as that person every single day. That's when new neural pathways are created and those limiting beliefs you once had about yourself start to melt away. They simply no longer relate to the person you're looking at in the mirror.

I'm constantly astounded by the limiting beliefs some of my clients have about their style and bodies. A limiting belief is a statement that you associate with yourself that's simply not serving you. We get these beliefs from friends, family, the media, and society. It becomes embedded in our brains and you start to believe it's true.

For example, here are some 'limiting beliefs' I hear all the time....

'I'm too old for fashion.' Says who? You are never too old to look and feel your best. The more fashionable your style, the younger you will seem. I'd almost go as far to say, fashion becomes even more important as you get older if you really want to be bolder and set yourself apart from your peers.

'I could never wear that.' I love it when my clients say that about something, it spurs me on to go out of my way to prove them wrong and I usually succeed. Cheeky I know, but it's true. You can't write off a whole category of clothing based on one experience; usually the case. There is always a solution, an alternative and when you find it, it's utterly liberating.

'I don't want to look like mutton dressed as lamb.' This is a problem so many women try so hard to avoid that they end up going to the other extreme and look frumpy. I'm not suggesting over-the-knee boots and leopard print mini dresses with pink faux fur coats, of course not, but don't stop yourself from pushing boundaries with your style as you get older for fear of being labelled 'mutton'. You can have your own individual flair and look sophisticated at the same time.

'I'm too big to be stylish.' Really? Do you actually believe that? I can show you many curvy ladies who look utterly fabulous. Size does not limit you from being stylish, that's on you.

'I need expensive items to look good.' Biggest load of rubbish ever, just saying.

'I wore it the first time round.' So what! It's different now. Why stop yourself from revisiting trends just because you wore it before? Who never saw the same movie twice? And that was literally the same. Fashion trends are cyclical, they come and go like passing clouds, during that time, you've grown older and changed too. Even if you didn't like it the first time round, you might find you bloody love it now.

Don't close your mind off to something before you've actually tried it on.

'I can't wear bright colours.' Oh yes you can. It's the oldest claim in the book. Everyone can wear bright colours, you just need to experiment to see which colours make you look and feel your best. We'll be digging deeper into this later on in the book.

'I don't suit prints.' A-ha, let's see about that. This is something I get told all the time and it's usually based on nothing. There are so many print options out there, I guarantee there is something that you will like. Lots of fun to be had with prints in Week 9, I can't wait for you to get there.

'I just don't have any sense of style.' Okay this may have been true up until now, but I am going to show you some simple building blocks to ensure you leave the house looking stylish every day. No one needs to know where you got it from, unless you tell them about this book. Actually, please do as that will really help me too. Sharing the love and all that.

Can you see how these limiting belief systems aka neural pathways are the foundation of our habits, how we act, in addition to how we think and feel.

When we focus on gratefulness and positive thoughts, we strengthen the pathways in our brain to feel "happy" and the reciprocal is true when we focus on pain and trauma. It is very important, therefore, to be mindful of our thoughts and to practise and strengthen the positive ones when they arise.

So your challenge for this week is to notice all the negative thoughts that come into your mind as you continue to wear your best outfits and bright lipstick, just like you did in week 1. Write them down in your journal and then underneath each one write a sentence that changes the negative statement into a more positive one. If you find this difficult, step into your alter ego, what would they say? Ava Storm would be having none of this silly nonsense that's for sure. It really helps whip any negative thoughts into touch, when I ask myself…what would Ava say?

For example:

Limiting belief: 'I'm too large to look good.'

New mantra: 'My clothes help to flatter and enhance my gorgeous curves.' Or in Ava's words: 'Honey, you are what you are, live with it, embrace it and make the most of it. You're unique and trust me when I say, no-body cares.' Got to love Ava, she's taking no prisoners.

Each morning when you wake up, read through the positive statements you've written and repeat in the mirror out loud every time a negative thought sneaks into your mind. By doing so you will subconsciously start to change the way you think about yourself, the way you speak to yourself and create a new neural positive pathway in your brain.

Style Challenge 1

Write down your limiting beliefs.

Once you've done that, take a break as it's never easy doing brain work. Don't stress if you can't think of them all at once, just add them to the list as and when something pops into your head. Next, make a cup of tea (why not) and when you're feeling a bit more refreshed I'd like you to revisit the photos you selected for the 'future' (RHS) section of your style board. Make a critical assessment. Have you played it safe and selected photos within the subconscious limitations you've set for yourself? Or have you truly let your mind soar and chosen photos that are beyond anything you could ever hope to achieve? That's where I want you to go. Don't hold yourself back, this is purely a visual exercise but an important one, as it will impact on all the steps to follow in this book and your transformation potential.

Style Challenge 2

Style board review.

Once you're done, come back and let's carry on. Feel free to take a break and come back to this tomorrow or in a few days. I don't want you to get too overwhelmed and throw in the towel. Hang in there, this work is hard as it requires you to be really honest with yourself but the payoff is huge.

> **"Don't let your limiting beliefs destroy your style dreams."**

As a stylist I see you in a totally different way to how you see yourself, my mind is not limited by your thoughts. My job is to not only put you in clothes that fit and flatter your shape but to flick that switch in your brain. The switch that's been OFF for a long time, that hasn't been activated because it's stuck down by your limiting beliefs. The most exciting part of this whole process is that I don't flick that switch, you do it all on your own. I just help to create an environment that enables you to have the confidence to do it.

Don't let your limiting beliefs destroy your style dreams. Start thinking of yourself as looking great all the time and leave me to help you to make those dreams a reality.

Ava says, repeat after me....
'I am limitless.'

Exciting! On a scale of 1 to 10, with 10 being the highest, how Bold are you feeling right now?

References: Wendy Suzuki : Change your brain, change your life

What you will need for next week:

- **Storage cubes for your bras and knickers.**

FOUNDATIONS OF A FLAWLESS FIT

It's Week 4,

almost 1 month into your transformation, how are your positive affirmations going? Are you surprised at how often a negative thought pops into your mind? We are so hard on ourselves it's ridiculous.

We don't even realise how often we put ourselves down until we start to be conscious of it. Keep journaling and exploring these negative thoughts, it helps to understand where they came from and why you feel that way about yourself. One thing's for sure, there is no place for limiting beliefs if your transformation from 'Bolder not Older' is going to be successful. So keep working on reprogramming these beliefs into new empowering ones and before you know it they will start to fade and hold less power over you.

You are almost halfway through your transformation, you've done the brain work, the visualisation and now you're going to work on building a strong foundation for your styling, starting with your shape.

There's no such thing as the perfect body. You may look at someone and think they have the perfect figure but in their mind all they see is their flaws, and I know this as I've styled women of all shapes and sizes and believe me when I say, no one is completely satisfied with their shape.

Imagine what life would be like if we all just loved our body shape no matter what? That's not to say we should sit back, relax and not bother to exercise or eat healthily, but be accepting of our limitations and empowered with knowledge and information on how to make the best out of what we have each and every day. This is the core of what this book is about, there are a lot of things we can't fundamentally change about ourselves, but there's a lot we can do to make us look and feel our best.

This chapter is all about defining your shape, embracing and moulding your curves, securing the foundation of any outfit with the correct underwear. I've set 5 style challenges for you this week. Don't stress if you don't manage to do all of them. Some involve booking appointments which you can schedule in the coming week, but try not to skip any challenges, as they are designed as important stepping stones in the journey towards being bolder.

But before we get on to that, let's have a moan…..we all love one of those and to be honest, it's important to get things off your chest once in a while. This is your moment to do that.

Having a wobble

Originally, under garments were constructed to create an hourglass figure and we've been endlessly obsessed by what body shape we are since. Yet given we are all unique and whether we like it or not asymmetrical – can we really fit our perceptions of ourselves into a type? Perhaps all we need to do is accept our imperfections, live with them and think of what solutions there are to minimise how we think we look and how we feel about how we look.

The first part of your style challenge this week is to be really honest with yourself about what you dislike about your shape. Knowing most women, you'll probably find this task really easy, ha! I'd like you to write down a list of all the areas of your body that you find most challenging to dress well. Get it off your chest girl, the

Style Challenge 1

bad, the flab... roll it all out once and for all. To get you going, I'll even have a go.....

- **I've never liked my knees.**
- **My legs are a few inches too short. Oh to be 5ft8.**
- **My once flat stomach now has a 'muffin top', thanks to two kids and middle age.**

I could go on, but you don't need to listen to all my bugbears, because they're irrelevant. As much as I would love to have long slim legs, I'm not held back by the fact that I don't, and I am totally accepting of the fact that I never will. I just style-it-out by wearing clothes that show off my best bits and make the most of the shape I am. And the older I've got the more I get my legs out. I now show off my knees and legs with pride, clever style choices help, but I've also stopped being held back by the things I can't control and focus instead on the things that I can like regular exercise to keep them toned as much as possible, and a little bit of fake tan always goes a long way.

It's good to identify the areas you wish you could change and then let's get to work altering how you perceive those areas and how others see you. No surgery required.

> My body bugbears are......get out your journal and write down all your body bugbears and then follow that up with all the things that you love about your body so you're not left hanging on a negative.

All done? Well done, now that's where the negativity ends. Take that piece of paper and bury or burn it, whichever works. Get rid, we're no longer focusing on what we dislike about our shape but rather taking a more practical approach by building a smooth foundation upon which to layer fabulous looks.

Out of shape

Shapewear has had a chequered history from the days of corsetry to cross your heart bras and the rigour of Spanx. For years women had to buy petticoats and slips for wearing under dresses and skirts, but the advent of anything goes (including bra burning) changed our relationship forever with under garments.

As the wonderful and dresser of many a Hollywood star, Edith Head said in her 1967 book *How to Dress For Success*, "dressing for success without a chapter on fashion's vitally important 'undercover' agents would be as ineffectual as an Ian Fleming thriller without James Bond. Just as Bond is the one who holds things together and shapes up the ultimate triumph, so too are your under-things the secret agents, shaping you for success. The most lavish and beautiful wardrobe in the world won't get you the job, the man, the social position or whatever else you desire if what you wear underneath it all is out of date or out of shape."

Or, I would add, not holding you up in the right places. The shape of your under garments are key to clothing hanging or fitting nicely. I'm not necessarily talking about matching bras and knickers, but items that will work wonders for you if you are worrying about your tummy or thighs. When women say to me, 'Oh I could never wear that!' my response is usually, yes you can, you just need the right support underneath.

But before we get on to new gen miracle shapers let's get down and dirty and take a look at what you've got to work with. You're going to do the big wardrobe detox in Week 6, but before you get on to that, I always think a good place to start is in your underwear drawer. Often an afterthought and most often never decluttered at all; by the time you've got through detoxing your wardrobe there will be no steam left to tackle your underwear collection. So, we're going to do it now, while you're feeling fresh and motivated.

Brief encounters

An often-neglected area of one's wardrobe – your knicker drawer, stash, or collection for want of a better word. Frequently rammed with items that never see the light of day. Date night knickers that get hauled out once a year at best, skimpy thongs that are lying low and far too many pants that are just that…pants! Your second style challenge this week is to get stuck in and streamline your underwear top to toe.

There is honestly nothing nicer than opening your underwear drawer and seeing everything beautifully lined up and compartmentalised as opposed to a big ball of lace and cotton jumbled together. My advice is invest in some fit for purpose storage that will slot into your drawers and separate your bras, socks and knickers so you can see exactly what you've got. When I invested in storage cubes for my underwear drawer, it gave me so much joy and satisfaction to be able to clearly see exactly what I have. A positive start to every day. Small things can make such a big difference.

Let's get stuck in.

Style Challenge 2

Consolidate your pants.

1 Take them all out and put them on your bed.

2 Do a quick sweep and chuck out any pieces that are overstretched, baggy, greying at the edges or dare I say it….holed.

3 Try on what's left and assess for fit and flatter factor. Do they make you feel good? I think it's important to feel good in one's underwear, that's the first step, the second is whether it provides a smooth finish underneath clothes. Underwear lines are a total distraction and will destroy an outfit. It's so important and something that's relatively easy to get right. A quick and easy way to assess is to try knickers on under leggings to assess VPL's and body lines.

4 Do a gap analysis to see what's missing. This may be easier to do once you've read all about the shapewear options available, but we often repeatedly buy the same thing forgetting that not all outfits require the same support. Variety is key.

5 Buy some storage cubes, easily available online, to store your briefs neatly so you can clearly see what you've got.

Next up….

Booby traps

Once you've gone through your knickers, move on to your bras. Do you really need so many? Are they all still a good fit and supportive? When did you last have a bra fitting? This is especially important when we hit the perimenopause as most women's breasts will change significantly during this transition to menopause.

The benefits of a well fitted bra are multifold, a good bra will:

- **Slim proportions, as it lifts breasts up, showing off your waist.**

- **Improve your posture; tighter bra straps help to prevent slouching.**

- **Boost confidence; your clothes will look better, and you'll feel more comfortable wearing them as a result.**

- **Improved health and wellbeing; a well-fitting bra that supports breasts perfectly will reduce back pain, skin irritation and chest pain. Particularly relevant for ladies with larger busts.**

There you have it, a good bra is a must. The question is do you have one?

Time to find out…

Systematically work through each of your bras, trying them on to see if they're holding you up in all the right places. Throw out anything that no longer fits properly or that is beginning to look faded, grey or worn.

Things to watch out for:

- Loose straps.
- Back strap already on the tightest notch.
- Under or overfilled cups.
- Discomfort: a bra should be supportive but like a second skin in terms of comfort.

Then invest in specialist bra storage cubes and pack what's left neatly back in your draw.

Style Challenge 3

Review your bra collection and store remaining in your new storage cubes.

I hope that was a satisfying and enlightening exercise.

Lastly, unless you've had one in the last 6 months, I'd like you to book in a bra fitting. It's so worth touching base to see if your bra is still doing you and your bust a good service. It won't cost you a thing but the price of wearing ill-fitting bras will take its toll on your confidence. Even if you don't think you need it, you've got nothing to lose by doing it and you might even find a new bra that's a much better fit.

Style Challenge 4

Book in for a bra fitting.

I have streamlined my bra wardrobe to include 2 bras, both neutral in tone, one strapless. I replace them both every six months and am always amazed at the difference in fit and comfort when I do. I couldn't afford to do that with a huge bra wardrobe, so I find streamlining it to two classic styles covers me for most dress situations. You may prefer to have a bigger selection of bra-styles, that's absolutely fine, but do make a point of trying them all on when you do your wardrobe detox twice a year for a fit check, replacing any that are past their best.

"If you have yet to unlock the magic that is modern shapewear, prepare to have your world rocked."

Shape lifting

Brilliant work on decluttering and embracing all the challenges this week, I know it may feel like you're still a long way off from transforming your look but this book isn't a crash diet in style. It's about making long-term, lasting changes to the way you think about your body and the clothing choices you make as a result. That's simply not going to happen overnight, which is why we're doing this as a 12-week programme. Working through this book systematically, taking on each of the weekly challenges, and embracing the change that starts to happen is going to result in a new you, more aligned with who you really are, confident, self-assured – bolder.

A little digression, as I think it's important to be reminded why you're doing this. We're currently in week 4 of the programme and it's very easy to lose a bit of motivation, keep trusting in the process and the results will be amazing and worth all the effort, no sweat required. I'm excited and I hope you are feeling it too?

Back to the business of shape and foundation building. Just to make the point here, the purpose of shapewear is to shape and smooth curves, not strive for skinny. The right shapewear can transform not only an outfit, but how you feel in an outfit, it's that extra 20% confidence boost you get when all our lumps and bumps are smoothed to perfection. Think of it as another secret weapon in your 'Bolder armoury'. And yes I know the shapewear of yesteryear was so unforgiving, suffocating, awkward (forget going to the loo) not to mention sweat inducing (just trying to get it on) and a bonafide passion killer. Fortunately technology has evolved and now you can achieve smoothness without suffocation or sacrificing comfort you'll be pleased to hear.

Shapewear of today is supposed to feel like a second skin not a suffocating corset. Not just saved for special occasions but worn everyday to smooth and skim your contours. They've become underwear essentials and should be part of your daily dressing toolkit. From cinching bodysuits to smoothing briefs, in fact they're so good you can wear them on top or underneath.

If you have yet to unlock the magic that is modern shapewear, prepare to have your world rocked. It's like someone took an iron to you and smoothed out every lump you have. It's like Photoshop for your living, breathing, three-dimensional body.

There's just one problem with this genre of wonder-garments: shapewear has gotten so popular that it now comes in a seemingly endless array of styles and fabrics, depending on which part of your body you want to disguise or even enhance, think bum enhancing shorts (yes really!!). How do you decide which will work best for your body and your wardrobe?

Here's my guide to choosing the best shapewear for you:

1. Stick to your size: Women often downsize for extra firmness but often that only causes bulges and discomfort, which can actually make you look bigger. A stylist tip is always stick to your normal size or even go up a size to avoid squashing and suffocating your organs and body parts. It's definitely worth going to a store or ordering some pieces online to try and to see what fits best on you. Sit down and walk around while you wear it to make sure that you feel comfortable and that the piece stays in place. You need to be able to eat and drink. We're aiming for shapewear that becomes part of your daily life, not just a one-off special occasion. You don't have to suffer to look and feel fabulous.

2. Support level: Opt for light to medium construction to smooth the lines.

Strong construction, ultra-slimming shapewear, will result in total figure transformation, which goes hand in hand with reduced comfort, this may be totally worth it for the right occasion, but it isn't sustainable every day. For the purposes of day to day smoothing, light comfort is what we're looking for. Medium compression levels are firmer than the light ones and may be suitable for casual events or evening outings. You can get a sense of the level of shaping by feeling the fabric. If it's lightweight and slips through your hands, it's most likely designed to simply smooth out targeted spots on your figure, perfect for day to day. Heavier pieces are usually armed with compression zones that will suck and tuck your body into shape. If unsure, look for a performance level on the packaging, or check out the clothing label. The higher the nylon content, the more a garment will alter your shape. The best check is always to try on and see how comfortable they feel. A bit like a pair of shoes, can you walk, run, and sit easily? Most importantly, can you breathe?

3. Tummy control: Even if you're not in the market for shapewear, I would urge you to consider tummy control briefs. Most women over the age of 40, even slim sized ladies, will benefit from smoothing and shaping in this area. The biggest benefit is avoiding the knicker line that cuts across the front of an outfit, usually just below the belly button, my biggest bug bear and so easily avoided. That doesn't mean you need to succumb to big pants, technology has moved on and you can get shaper briefs with a thong or a mid-thigh short that look good without your clothes on, but also remove all VPL's. Thongs are definitely an undergarment you should select one or two sizes up in to prevent any feelings of discomfort in the nether regions. Go for light support and nude fabrics for versatility and a smooth finish.

4. High waist-it: Ideal for love handles or muffin tops you don't want anyone else to know about. Look for versions that go right up to your bra-line or even hook onto your bra line for added support if needed. Alternatively, a bodysuit is a seamless choice to layer over bras or even wear without a bra depending on your bust size.

5 Tone the legs: Try tights with in-built shapewear. The first problem with wearing tights over shapewear is that you're putting nylon blends next to each other, which will cause your tights to shift to the side. Second, this creates an extra layer in the thigh region, which could cause seams to show through your clothes. Look instead for shapewear tights that have compression zones that shape the tummy, thighs and bum area while offering the seamless and sleek sheer you get from a regular pair of tights. Practical and comfortable at the same time. If you don't want to wear tights then choosing trousers with a thicker fabric and added stretch, will do the job just as well for you.

6 The bodysuit: This traditional shape has come a long way from the triathlon style cycling outfit so many women used to persevere with. The bodysuit is popular because it creates a head-to-toe streamlined shape, saving you the trouble of finding separate top and bottom pieces that work. The all-over coverage is also a plus if you want to minimise a larger chest because it has a flattening effect, like that of many sports bras. But, if that doesn't work for you, choose a bodysuit that's cut around the bust and let your bra do the work of supporting your chest. Personally, I prefer the new-gen bodysuits that look like a leotard, have enough stretch to support a small to medium bust and are easy to wear day to day. Not for everyone, but definitely worth a try as the comfort and smoothing effect are second to none. Plus they can also be worn as a top, perfectly for layering under blazers for a seamless look and you don't need to worry about waistbands rolling up.

7 Cooler options: Shapewear is typically made of nylon and spandex, both synthetic fabrics that don't breathe. That's great in cooler climates, where you want to retain as much body heat as possible, but in the warmer months, it makes you more prone to sweat, not ideal if you're in full flush. Fortunately, several brands sell summer shapewear, lighter versions of their original products designed with breathability in mind. Japan-based Wacoal offers a wide selection of styles in its 'Cool Definition' line. The fabric used for this, includes cotton for moisture absorption and breathability and microfiber for odour control.

8 Budget friendly: You don't have to spend a fortune. There are lots of options on the market to suit most budgets. Start with one or two items and gradually build as you start to enjoy the benefit of good, comfortable support. No more photo's catching you at a bad angle, we've all had those! In fact, I'd almost go as far to say that the first thing on your shopping list should be shapewear before you invest in any new clothes.

If you're unsure which style of shapewear to go for, book yourself in for a fitting like you would for a bra, but ask for advice on shapewear instead. Whether you embrace any of this advice and invest in shapewear or not, please be mindful of underwear lines. Always check your outfit out in 3-D when you look in the mirror in case there's anything on show that shouldn't be.

Style Challenge 5

> Try on some shapewear. Order online if you don't have time to go shopping. Try some of the options mentioned above to see how they make you feel and more importantly how it changes the way your clothes look on your body. No diet, no gym, just shape.

"Great underwear is the foundation of confidence."

Phew, I appreciate that there was a lot of talk about underwear, that's because it's that important, yet often the most neglected area of our wardrobes.

I will say it again, and probably not for the last time, if the foundation fits well, anything you layer on top has the best chance of looking good. Compromise the quality and fit of your underwear and everything you wear will look second best. So, don't skimp on the advice in this chapter.

Do as many of the tasks as you can and really invest in a shapewear collection that you can rely on for any occasion or outfit. If you're up for it, I'd like you to start wearing some form of shaping underwear everyday just to get into the habit of doing it and journal how it makes you feel.

See you in Week 5.

APPLES AND PEARS, WHO ACTUALLY CARES

5 weeks in and I know what you're thinking,

when does the real styling start? Now is the answer. This is where we start to adapt your dream style to suit you...

We may need a few tweaks here and there but if you really want to be bolder the first step is to believe and the second step is to understand your body shape, but not be limited by a list of dos and don'ts. It's when we get bogged down by what we think we should and shouldn't wear for our shape or age that any hope of being bolder in one's style choices flies out the window.

You are what you are

I think the biggest secrets to great style are made up of two elements.

Point 1, Acceptance. Acceptance of your shape, your curves, your height, your tummy, your everything, whatever your size and not being limited by your shape. Looking good has zero to do with how slim you are and everything to do with how you feel about your body. As Ava always says to me when I'm over analysing myself in front of the mirror… **'Darling, you are what you are, but no one else needs to know, unless you choose to show them.'**

Which brings me nicely onto point 2, Knowledge. Knowing how to mould your shape to perfection with a great outfit is your arme secrète (secret weapon). That's why this chapter is so important, not to label your shape but to learn how to make your shape your greatest asset.

> "To be beautiful means to be yourself. You don't need to be accepted by others. You need to accept yourself."
>
> **Tich Nhat Hanh,** Buddhist monk, Author and peace activist.

No one cares

When I work with my clients, I never label their body shape, unless they specifically ask me to. Let's face it no one wants to be labelled an 'Apple' or 'Inverted Triangle'. They're labels that immediately make you feel odd, abnormal and out of balance. It's obviously important for me as a stylist to be able to assess someone's body shape, but I do all of that in my head. As we know no two body shapes are the same, some are tall, others short. Some smaller in size, others larger. Plus, we may start off as one shape when we're younger, but then miraculously appear to morph into something quite different as the peri and then menopause work their transformation havoc, oh yes, I know all about that. Life loves to keep us on our toes, doesn't it? It's exactly why midlife is the perfect time to refresh the way you dress and the clothes that you keep in your wardrobe.

There are so many elements that come into styling a shape that one set of rules won't fit everyone, and as a result, labelling often ends up causing more confusion than clarity. One common denominator amongst most midlife women I meet is the waist expansion that seems to go hand in hand with the hormone roller coaster. It's the number one thing that a lot of women struggle with and hate. So much so that they'll do anything to hide it away. It's the only thing they see when looking in the mirror and it becomes the focus around which they base most of their clothing choices.

All because we don't want to draw attention to our flaws. Well I have news for your girlfriend….nobody cares. Literally nobody….but you. Everyone is too busy wrapped up in their own heads to take any notice of how big your tummy is.

Individuality is your superpower

Instead of compartmentalising you into a shape, as let's face it darling, you're different, I'm going to focus on the body challenges we all face and give you my top tips, little things you can do to fix them or as I like to say 'style-them-out' so they become less of a focus. How to minimise a belly, how to flatter a large bust, how to slim your thighs and conceal those

> "Being bolder is being resolute, unwavering when it comes to your style and image. Knowing how to dress well for your shape and size and then stamping your style identity all over it."

dreaded bingo wings (awful term, but it serves its descriptive purpose).

The positive in all of this is that your clothes are your secret weapon to looking and feeling fabulous, to living a bolder life. Looking your best is not about the size or shape you are, and all about having the right clothes. This means that you have the power and ability to look amazing, to be bolder, no matter what. If you've ever seen any of the makeover

TV shows I've hosted, I have styled and masterminded the transformation of ladies who felt decidedly worse for wear to begin with and end up looking like a million dollars; trust me when I say, anyone, including you, has the potential to look incredible – you just need better clothes, the compulsion to try new things and the confidence to wear them.

What I really want you to embrace from now on, is to not let whatever part of your body you dislike hold you back from trying new things. Ava would never let her image hold her back. Allow your alter ego to support you through this stage if it feels daunting. Often, we are most reticent to experiment on the areas we are most self-conscious about. But hey, what's the worst that can happen? It doesn't work, you move on! I'd rather you gave something a try than stop yourself because you think it won't work, remember those new cognitive pathways we've been working on? The best items are often the pieces you least expect. Don't let your bust or waist hold you back from discovering your true style potential. Be bold and just go for it, you have nothing to lose.

Use my top tips below to help boost your confidence in the areas you are most self-conscious about.

But before I start, I just want to make the point that sometimes what works in principle, doesn't always work in reality. What I want you to do is take each of these tips and just give them a go. If something doesn't work, fine, feel free to bin it, but please try before you decide.

How to style a tummy

1 Shape-it: Wearing the right shapewear can make all the difference. We spent a lot of time exploring this last week and hope you agree that investing in a few pieces really helps to smoothen out your silhouette, especially the areas you are most self-conscious about, works like a magic eraser. A waisted brief with extra shaping across the front is my go-to for shaping and smoothing; you may prefer a body suit or something else. You don't need to wear shapewear every day but trust me when I say it's a game changer. If you haven't already invested in a couple of pieces, now is most definitely the time.

2 Use print to disguise: I know this may not be something you do or even want to do but in my experience nothing works as well as a bold print when it comes to camouflaging your midline. In fact, the bolder the print the better. Lots of print style tips coming in week 9.

3 Ruching works wonders: Tops or dresses with stretch and ruching across the stomach will not only disguise but also define a shape. It's got to be seen to be believed, so many women are too scared to try something in fear of it not looking good, but just imagine if you face the fear and the result is amazing. Try it!

4 Find your midline: Your waist is roughly one inch above your belly button or the narrowest part of your tummy. Even if you have a large or broad waistline it's still important to define that waist, as it will help to balance your proportions. If you're nervous about drawing attention to your waist, wear loose dresses that have a line across the midline, creating a waist, and a tiered skirt. This helps to elongate the bottom half of your body and make the middle and top part appear proportionately smaller.

5 Avoid head to toe black: When you feel self-conscious of your body, especially your waistline it's very easy to hide it (or think you're hiding it) under a black canvas. But, in reality, you're fooling no one and you're only making yourself feel worse. In fact, an all-black outfit can make you look larger, not smaller.

6 Tailoring can be a miracle worker: Choose clothes that add shape as opposed to a shapeless alternative. I find tailoring works like a dream when you're trying to disguise a tummy. Mid to high waist trousers will hold you in and a tailored blazer will instantly define a waist. My top tip here is to size down on the blazer if you can and wear it open rather than closed. Closing a blazer creates more of a square shape whereas when you wear it open you create a vertical line down the middle which is much more slimming. If you really want to disguise the tummy, opt for a colourful suit e.g. cobalt blue and layer a black cami or blouse underneath, the eye will be attracted to the blue colour and the tummy will be concealed but your waist will be defined. For the more adventurous, or when you become adventurous, you can swap the black cami for a blue one for full colour wow head to toe. Yes you will draw attention when you walk in the room but isn't that what all women want; to look good and be visible? I promise you, deep down you really do.

7 Colour-in your imperfections: I'm going to be banging on about colour a lot in this book as it's my number one passion when it comes to fashion, but also having transformed many men and women over the years, I have proved over and over again that bright colours, lift moods and change lives. If you want people to stop commenting about your weight, give them something else to talk about. If you don't want to be described as the large lady in the corner, let them talk about the gorgeous lady in green. Trust me when I say a colourful outfit is your body's best disguise. No one is looking at your curves when you're wearing a vibrant colour. A bucket load of ideas on how to style colour are waiting for you in Week 8. So don't worry if this isn't an area you're comfortable with, I will get you there.

8 The art of diversion: If you're easing into wearing colour, then this is a good place to start. Put the colour on the area you like the most and a darker shade or neutral on the part you want to hide. So if you're conscious of your tummy, go for a pop of colour in your trousers and team with navy, forest green, burgundy or even black on top. I like to keep it tonal with the brighter and darker tone of the same colour mixed together for an effortless style, but I'll go more into that later.

9 Tucked in or out: In my experience tucked in with a slight blouson or partially tucked in (side tuck) usually looks better than untucked especially if it's a loose unfitted top. This may feel uncomfortable as a concept but it really works. Usually best with a high waisted skirt or trousers. Try it and see how this feels as an idea.

10 Wrap it up: A wrap dress or wrap-style top is a style saviour when it comes to disguising a tummy. If you take nothing else from this book, take the wrap. Especially flattering if you've got a good bust as well. If it was up to me I'd say go for a wrap with a print as you're going to get a double whammy flatter factor.

11 Zip placement: Flat fronted trousers with a side zip help to smooth and flatten a tummy without adding the bulk of a button and zip in the middle which just draws the eye to the centre point of a tummy. Alternatively go for an elasticated back to a trouser with a flat front for larger sizes.

12 When all else fails, add a belt: I mean it, it may not seem logical but just because you have curves doesn't mean you can't wear a belt. A belt is especially important if you're wearing a voluminous dress; avoid looking like a tent and add a belt to define a waist and balance proportions. The shorter you are, the slimmer the belt should be to avoid foreshortening your torso. Also great when added at the waist over high waisted trousers or skirts.

"Style is not about fitting into a mould but embracing what makes you unique. Every body shape has its own beauty, and the key to great style is enhancing your natural silhouette with confidence and creativity."

How to style a large bust

1 **Open the neckline:** For large busts, an open neckline is always more flattering. A shirt unbuttoned slightly, a scooped, v-neck or cowl neck top help to separate and draw attention away from the width of the bust to the breast bone / middle point of your cleavage. This doesn't mean you should live in a v-neck dress, t-shirt or jumper, but opting for a slightly unbuttoned blouse, shirt or shirt dress is always a winner. If you find buttons tend to pull across the bust, then a wrap top or dress will totally circumvent this issue.

2 **Brasserie perfection:** I've said it already and I'll say it again, a well fitted bra will do wonders for your style and your cleavage. In fact, it's the first thing you should do, if you haven't got around to it yet.. Doesn't matter what you wear, it simply won't look as good with a poor fitting bra.

3 **Embrace your bust:** If you're really self-conscious about your bust, opt for a darker shade like navy, teal, maroon, burgundy, mustard or forest green on top instead of a bright. If possible, avoid black where possible. Remember, this book is about making you look 'Bolder, not Older' and black can be very ageing on your skin.

4 Print to the rescue: Print really can work wonders on a large bust, avoid a symmetric print like horizontal stripes and go for something more haphazard in design. Mid-sized prints are ideal (too small can feel frumpy and too big a print can overwhelm and have the opposite effect), choose the type of print to suit your style; floral, geometric, polka dots, animal print and vertical stripes all work well. If you're worried about drawing attention to your bust with a print, go for a dress with an all over pattern or a co-ord to elongate proportions.

5 Layer your lines: A very easy way to make a bust appear smaller is to reduce the volume of bust on show. This can be done by layering a blazer or jacket over a top or dress. Two options here, either layer a coloured jacket over a black cami or top or wear a printed top under a coloured or neutral blazer. Perhaps start with the first option to see how this feels and move on to the second option as your confidence builds.

6 Size down: Jackets are best worn open to create that long vertical line down the middle of the body. I often suggest my client's size down on a jacket so that it holds its shape when worn open. Buttoning up a jacket instantly squares off your shape.

7 Double vs single: When it comes to jackets and coats, single breasted is the best bet to create a longer v-neckline which moves the eye away from the bust and lengthens proportions.

8 A fine art: The finer the knit or weave the more slimming on a large bust. Avoid heavy, bulky knits that will only add unnecessary volume.

Quick tips to style a small bust

1 **Pump up the volume:** Invest in a bra that shapes, lifts and gives your bust a bit of a boost.

2 **Raise it up:** High necklines will make a small bust look fuller.

3 **Ruffled:** Blouses with ruffle detailing across the bust will add much needed volume.

4 **One sided:** Asymmetric necklines are hugely flattering for a small bust.

5 **Embellish:** Layer a statement necklace over a shirt or blouse to add volume and draw the eye up.

6 **Bold prints:** A statement horizontal stripe for example will help broaden a small bust.

7 **Statement sleeves:** Oversized balloon or statement sleeves will add volume to a small bust and chest.

8 **Texturise:** The more texture on top the better. Chunky knits, embellished tops, faux fur, velvet etc. will all add volume and conceal a small bust.

How to style curvy hips

Now this advice applies to all sizes, doesn't matter what your dress size is, if your hips are wider than your shoulders, they're curvy, and most likely something you tend to focus on hiding when you get dressed. Here are my top style tips to flatter this area:

1 **Strip back the volume:** Most often when clients feel self-conscious of their hips and bum they try to cover it with lots of fabric. Totally natural instinct, I get it. You don't want anyone to notice so you drown it in volume. My advice is to strip back the volume and embrace your curves. If you are tall 5 ft 8' and above you can get away with wearing more volume on your legs but anyone shorter and it throws off all proportion and just makes this area look wider. A better solution is a straight leg, boot leg, slim fit, cigarette leg, capri or flare, the aim is to pick something that's fitted on the hip and thigh area. Doesn't matter too much if there's volume below that, unless you're petite in which case trousers that are narrow/taper around the ankle are a better choice. I know it might sound uncomfortable if you're currently living in wide leg trousers, but try and experiment with a slimmer fit this week.

2 **A few extra inches:** As I mentioned above, the taller you are the more volume you can carry off. Whether you're set on your wide leg trousers (totally ok btw, I want you to pick and choose the pieces you take away from this book and personalise it for you), or keen to embrace less volume, a few extra inches really helps slim down hips and lengthen legs. I know many of us are wedded to our flats thanks to the pandemic, but there are shoe options out there that will give you a lift and also be comfortable. You don't have to run around in stilettos. A block heel, an ankle strap, or ankle boots for example all provide support, comfort and some much-needed extra inches. If you're shorter than 5 ft 8'', I challenge you to find and try a pair of shoes with a heel. It doesn't need to be a high heel, any heel is a good start, kitten, block, platform or wedge.

3 Waisted: The best way to slim your hips is to draw attention to your waist. Always choose high waisted trousers and skirts where possible as it naturally lengthens legs and shows off a waist. Similarly, a waisted belt is an essential styling tool when diverting attention away from the hip area. Choose any width of belt as long as it is waisted.

4 Reverse psychology: Now bear with me on this. A completely logical way to disguise your hips and legs is with black, navy or dark coloured plain trousers or skirts and wearing print and colour on top to divert the eye upwards. This totally works but it can lead to formulaic and boring style. You can absolutely wear colour and print on this area, but make sure you balance it with a colour or print on top so your legs aren't the feature of the look. Does that make sense? For example, red trousers teamed with a black blouse, the focus is going to be on the trousers and therefore you'll feel your hips are on show. Red trousers with a leopard print blouse, the focus is on the outfit not your hips. I'll be covering off lots of tips on styling colour and print in Week 8 and 9 for more examples on this. So have a play with this as a concept now and we'll be deep diving into this in a few weeks' time.

5 Symmetry: Another great way to elongate your legs and proportionately slim your thighs is to match your shoe colour to your trousers to avoid creating a breakpoint. Red trousers with red heels or boots for example.

6 Top to toe: Another brilliant way of elongating proportions and slim hips is to wear one colour top to toe. Straightforward when it comes to a dress but apply it to separates as well by wearing the same colour top and bottom plus accessories like your shoes, if you really want to push the boat out, which I know you do; there is no holding you back now! See colour chapter, Week 8, for more tips on how to do this well.

7 Structure is supportive: The best way to flatter curvy hips is to mould the curves. Go for trousers and skirts that add structure and shape, not ones that just hang off your silhouette. You may feel self-conscious at first as your hips will be on show, but for all the right reasons. Embrace your sexy curves, don't hide them under layers of loose material. Thicker, stretchier fabrics on trousers and skirts will be more reliable than silky, satiny options.

Match your shoe colour to your trousers to avoid creating a breakpoint. Red trousers with red heels or boots for example.

8 Fitted or loose: When styling a blazer or jacket, a tailored fit is essential. Avoid straight loose cuts like boyfriend styles which will square off proportions. The length really doesn't matter too much, as long as it's shaped or fitted at the waist. Only thing I'd say to be mindful of is to avoid a blazer that sits on the widest point of your hips.

9 Tucked in: When it comes to tops, there is a tendency to wear longer length blouses and tops that cover the hip and bum area. I totally get why you would do this but it's not the most flattering choice. The more the curve of your hip is embraced the more in proportion and better you will look. So any tops or blouses should be tucked in where possible, if that feels too much, try a side tuck to create some shape and show off your waist. If you want to wear a kaftan or longer line top, add a belt to create shape and balance proportions.

10 The topline: Another easily avoidable bugbear of mine, and one you will be aware of by now, visible underwear lines, especially when the top of knickers sit at the same point as the widest part of your hip line. It's an instant focal point and so easily avoided with a high waisted brief. Whether you opt for a thong, french knickers (boy shorts) or classic pants, make sure the band of your knickers sits at the same point as the top of your skirt or trousers and doesn't fall below and create a crease.

How to style bingo wings

Simple styling choices can totally resolve this area, making it a non-issue and helping you to feel comfortable and confident in what you're wearing, and it doesn't mean you have to cover them up.

1 Flute-it: A fluted sleeve will fall softly over the upper arm area, providing coverage but not clinging. Just enough fabric to conceal whilst showing off the slimmest part of your arm.

2 The cold shoulder: Tops with a dropped sleeve exposing the top of the shoulder whilst disguising the upper arm are a dream come true for disguising this area. They add a level of softness and femininity whilst providing enough coverage to boost confidence.

3 Cut-away: Cutaway shoulders are where the fabric is cut away from the top of the shoulder towards the neck e.g. halterneck or racerback style tops. This shows off more arm and shoulder which might feel like a conflict but by doing this you add extra length to the arms and draw the eye towards the neck and away from the upper arm area. It's worth a try even if it feels out of your comfort zone.

4 Off the shoulder: Bandeau style tops work well to expose flesh on the shoulder line whilst disguising upper arms at the same time. A great choice if you're self-conscious of this area.

5 Sheer love: A way to add a bit of coverage without adding bulk is to go for sheer fabrics that skim over arms, concealing enough whilst still adding femininity to a look.

6 Wrist action: Making your wrists a feature with bracelets or even a statement bag will draw the eye away from the top of the arms, particularly useful when wearing shorter sleeve tops. So much of great style is the art of diversion, concealing and only revealing the parts you want to show off.

7 Loosen up: Sleeves that fall with movement are more flattering than those that cling.

8 Neck first: A statement neckline is a brilliant way of diverting attention away from arms. A bold piece of jewellery like a necklace or earrings, embellished details such as a flower corsage, oversized bow or ruffles will help to create a focal point and feature. Not generally recommended for larger bustlines but as always, worth experimenting with new concepts and ideas as so often the least expected, work wonders.

Style Challenge 1

> This week's challenge is to pick the areas above that you find most challenging to dress well and experiment with these tips to see what works. Only focus on the tips that are relevant to you.

Don't worry if you don't have all the options at hand. Make a note of anything you need that you'd like to try so we can add that to your shopping list in week 12. Most importantly this week, I'd like you to just have a play, experiment with the tips using what you already have in your wardrobe, to see what resonates and works best.

Trust me when I say this is an easier week in terms of your time and effort required, purposefully so.

Next week we are going to take a deep dive into where all your skeletons truly lie, you guessed it... your wardrobe.

What you will need for next week:

- **A standalone rail:** this is useful for taking sections out of your wardrobe and sorting through it. Wardrobes are often small, cramped and dark and not always easy to see what you've got. Having a separate rail to hand makes the process less messy and frustrating. Make sure you invest in a sturdy one as you're going to be using it a lot from now on.

- **Vacuum bags:** very useful for storing away last season's clothes you won't be wearing for another 6 months.

- **Storage boxes:** for other unseasonal items like shoes etc that can't be vacuum packed.

- **A full-length mirror:** if you don't have one in your bedroom, it's time to get one.

- **Bin liners:** for items that are going to be sold, sent to the charity shop or into the recycling.

- **Sticky labels and a pen:** to label bin liners 'charity' or 'resale'.

- **Slimline hangers:** to replace your existing hangers as they take up a lot less space. Also useful to have on your rail for items that tend to be folded not hung.

THE GREAT CLOSET CLEANOUT

week 6

You're almost halfway there.

Well done on sticking with this process, it's going to be the best thing you've ever done. I know it feels like a lot of grind and not much fashion at the moment, but we're building a solid foundation from the ground up. The biggest mistake most people make with their style is only focusing on the bits people see and not creating a firm structure behind it.

Follow this process correctly and you'll look fabulous for life, not just an occasion. This week we are going to dig out all the skeletons in your closet and then some. We all have them, that pair of jeans you haven't been able to fit into for ten years but live in hope that someday you miraculously will. That horrific jumper your mother-in-law gave you for Christmas which you feel compelled to keep in case she pops round for tea. Our cupboards are full of secrets, past loves and past lives. Now's the time to move on and start living for the moment and working towards creating that bold new style that's on your vision board.

We are going to do a deep dive into your wardrobe, it's going to take time, so make sure you set aside a full morning and afternoon to get properly stuck in and ideally finish the job in a day, or focus on a section a day to spread the load and keep your energy levels up.

We'll be:

- **Decluttering**
- **Editing**
- **Streamlining**
- **Tidying**

It might sound like a boring task but trust me when I say this is going to be the most liberating, fulfilling exercise you've done in a long time. You'll finally be able to see the wood from the trees and have a wardrobe of clothes that make you shine. Even if you're left with only a few pieces you really love, it's a start, and we're going to build on this foundation – so don't worry, it may feel daunting but by the end of this week you'll be halfway through your transformation process already.

The Why

Do you open your wardrobe in the morning and smile?

Can you clearly see what you have?

Do you feel inspired to try new combinations out of the interesting pieces you have in your cupboard?

Are you able to instantly choose an outfit that makes you feel good?

No? Then this chapter will change your life.

Having a streamlined and clutter free wardrobe will take years of stress out of your life, for so many reasons:

Mood lifter

Life is short! The purpose of living is to savour and enjoy every moment as much as possible, yet our lives are cluttered with daily irritants; things that instantly put us in a bad or below par mood every day. For example: The bottom of the kitchen drawer keeps falling out, you've been meaning to get it fixed, of course you have, but for whatever reason (time, money etc) it hasn't been done. In the bigger scheme of life, it's nothing, but in reality, it's a daily aggravator. That thing that can instantly put you in a grump each and every morning when you have a run in with the kitchen drawer. The same goes for your wardrobe, it's an item in your home that you interact with every day, sometimes two or three times a day. It's up there with your kitchen and bathroom in terms of how much you use it. Yet so many of us never invest any time and money into creating a wardrobe space which not only looks streamlined and calming, but one where you can clearly see exactly what you've got! Instead, we throw open the cupboard doors each morning and instantly feel stressed trying to figure out what the hell to wear or even find something in the cluttered chaos, resulting in a below par outfit choice and a self-esteem blow. As the years go by it gets harder to look in the mirror, like what you see and believe you still have the opportunity and potential to conquer your dreams. One of the reasons you feel this way is because of the daily tasks that drag you down. Getting dressed is one of those, it shouldn't be and it certainly won't be once you've finished this book, but in reality for most people it really is. The main issue is your wardrobe, not your midline.

Release your demons

There are often a lot of emotions hanging in your wardrobe, some welcome, most not. The outfit you wore the first time you met your husband; happy memory but does it need to take up space in your closet? That very expensive pair of trousers you impulse bought and have never worn. Shedding the demons in your closet is never an easy thing, but you will feel liberated once you have; your closet will be cleansed of any negative messages that drag you down every time you're in search of something to wear.

You do not need to be defined by your past mistakes, remove the evidence, the reminders and free your mind and spirit to be the person you deserve to be.

Reduce overwhelm

Too many clothes give you too much choice. Why be faced with endless options in the morning? Our brains can only cope with so many stimuli at once which can lead to 'decision fatigue' and poor choices. One of the many reasons why people only wear 20% of their wardrobes 80% of the time.

Save money

How many times have you bought something only to realise you already have it. When you go through the process of systematically decluttering your wardrobe you will get a clear picture of what you really need and allow you to make the most of this process.

Above all, it will be impossible or quite frankly pointless investing in a new look, if you're simply going to stuff the new inspiration in with the old memories. Very soon they too will become part of the daily source of aggravation.

This daily cycle stops now! It is time my gorgeous friend, to get your hands stuck in and declutter your closet.

Essential Prep

Like any big project, success lies in the planning not the execution; a fresh cup of tea, coffee, glass of water or whatever drink you prefer..

Before you throw yourself into the deepest darkest recesses of your wardrobe, and to do the wardrobe edit well, there are a few things which will help to make the process more efficient and effortless. I've mentioned them already but here they are again:

- **Standalone rail**
- **Vacuum bags**
- **Storage boxes**
- **Full-length mirror**
- **Bin liners**
- **Sticky labels and a pen**
- **Slimline hangers**

Style Challenge 1

Prep your essentials.

Diary Management

The next step is to get your diary out and block half a day to tackle your detox. Now if your wardrobe is bulging you may need a few days, so allocate the appropriate amount of time in your diary to do it properly, so you don't feel rushed and pressured to get it done. I would suggest it takes on average 3–4 hours but as soon as you find your concentration dipping, you start to feel overwhelmed or unable to make decisions, you need to stop and pick it up again tomorrow.

Trust me when I say this is a bit of a messy process. You'll be going through sections in your wardrobe and creating piles of clothes for various destinations such as resale, charity shop or recycling bin. What you don't want is for the time you've allocated and most likely underestimated, to pass, leaving your bedroom or dressing room looking like a hand grenade exploded! This will only create more stress and inevitably, most of the items carefully allocated to piles will get thrown back into your wardrobe in exasperation. So if you have a lot of clothes to get through, approach this process in bite sized chunks. Perhaps it's an hour or two in the evenings and you focus on one section a day. More on this to come.

Seasoning

Once you've got your detox scheduled in your diary and before you start, I want you to take out any items that you're unlikely to wear in the current season. By season I mean the summer or winter season. If you're decluttering in spring/summer you want to remove any winter items from your wardrobe that you won't be wearing for the next six months. This includes:

- **Coats / jackets**
- **Gloves**
- **Winter hats**
- **Scarves**
- **Jumpers / knits**
- **Winter trousers and skirts**
- **Boots**
- **Ski-wear**
- **Thermal underwear, etc.**

If you're decluttering in winter you'll need to remove all your summer clothes such as:

- **Summer blouses**
- **Shorts**
- **Dresses**
- **Beachwear and swimsuits**
- **Sandals and flip-flops**
- **Hats**
- **Summer bags**
- **Summer jackets, etc.**

Place all clothing items in one of the vacuum bags you've invested in and seal them up according to instructions. Shoes and boots that aren't relevant for the current season should also be packed away. I put all my shoe boxes in a large plastic box and store them in the loft out of the way. You can also just stack your individual shoe boxes if it's easier.

Next, move all unseasonal items out of your bedroom, unless storing under your bed, but most definitely out of your wardrobe. If you have a loft or under-stairs storage that's the ideal place to keep them.

Just by moving unseasonal items out of your wardrobe should immediately lighten the load and create space in your closet. If it hasn't, then honey, you've got your work cut out but fear not, it can be done and trust me when I say this will be the most liberating, cleansing thing you've done in years.

Style Challenge 2

Move all your non-seasonal items out of your wardrobe.

The How

It's time to get stuck in, fresh cup of tea made, diary blocked, rail at the ready? Let's go.

Sectioned

First thing I want you to do is sort all your clothes into sections. For example, get all your jeans together, your trousers and your dresses. Don't worry too much at this stage about casual vs smart dresses, that comes later. Just group like-items together. A lot of my clients have their wardrobe spread over different locations/rooms for space. If that's the case and you've got some dresses in one wardrobe and some in another, then consolidate them all in one place together. You may need to move another section of items e.g. blazers to another location in order to do this. Where the various sections are doesn't matter, as long as all your clothes are sorted into like-items, then you're good to go.

Style Challenge 3

Group your clothes into like items.

The Big Sort

Well done! This is an important step in the process as it instantly gives you perspective of where the imbalances in your wardrobe lie. Lots of jeans and hardly any trousers for example? We tend to overbuy the things we like, to the point where I often find clients have duplicates of the same item without even realising.

Next, I want you to pick a section, let's stick with jeans as that's a pretty universal area in most of our wardrobes. You've already grouped them all together, now I want you to take them out and hang them on the rail. If you keep your jeans folded in your wardrobe, hang each one up on one of the slimline hangers you prepped with your rail.

Take a step back and observe the picture. What do you see? Any similarities, duplicates, too many of one colour or style? Before you start editing a section, I think it's good to get perspective of what some of your shopping habits are. What are the things you buy on repeat, time and again. Make a note in your journal, so you can remind yourself to avoid doing this in the future.

Now I want you to edit this section down. Read the prompts below to help you think about whether something should stay or go so it's considered and thoughtful. No need to be rash and impulsive. The aim of this exercise is to keep the pieces you love, that make you look good and most importantly feel good, but also fill a gap in your wardrobe. Those basic pieces, like a classic white shirt that don't necessarily

get us excited, but they can be a useful building block within an outfit.

The Section Edit

Round 1

I want you start editing this section down now, by removing any items that you know:

- **Don't fit. Take out anything too big or too small.**
- **Don't suit you anymore or perhaps they never did. That impulse buy with a friend, that sale bargain that still has the label on. We've all been there, don't beat yourself up, it's time to move on.**
- **You never wear. Whatever the reason it's taking up valuable space.**

I don't want you to overthink or linger on this. Be quite matter of fact and emotionally detached as you do this. Does it fit: yes or no. Do you like it: yes or no.

Place any 'No's' on the discard pile or even better, place them in the designated bin liner 'Charity', 'Resell', 'Recycle' or 'Bin' immediately. This should reduce the amount on your rail by up to a third and should take no longer than half an hour per section.

Note: if you're unsure about an item at this point, just place it back on your rail for round 2.

Style Challenge 4

Go through a section, decluttering as you go.

Round 2

Well done, that wasn't too difficult, was it?

You're now looking at your slightly edited rail. The only things remaining on your rail are either items you love and wear and items you're not 100% sure about; totally fine by the way to be unsure about some things, in fact I'd expect it; that's where round 2 comes in.

Divide what's left on your rail into items you 100% love and want to keep and those you're in two minds about. Next, go item by item through the undecided section on your rail and try it on. Think about all the things you learnt about flattering your shape in Week 5, and honestly critique each item according to its flatter-factor on a scale of 1 to 5. 5 being super flattering, and 1 making you feel unstylish and frumpy.

It's important you stand in front of a full-length mirror to really get a true perspective. Give the item its best chance, style it with a top, nothing looks good if you're half naked with your belly hanging out, adding a pair of heels often helps too, but the harder you have to work to make something look semi-decent or vaguely good is a clear indication that its not worthy of a coveted space in your wardrobe.

Then it's a matter of deciding which throw-out pile or bin liner it should go in: charity or resell? If it's in good condition and was an investment purchase, you will definitely be able to sell it on. Any money generated can be invested back into your wardrobe, but we'll get on to that.

Once the item has either been 'discarded' or placed back on the rail it's time to try the next piece on your rail. Now don't stress if this seems like a laborious process, I've explained it in detail here but you'll find you'll start slow, possibly overthinking everything and then you'll become a lot more decisive and accelerate as a result.

Once you've been through all the 'unsure' pieces on your rail you should have reduced the total items on your rail by at least another third, if not more. If not, it might be worth quickly going through the section again to see if you really need to keep all those items you've selected.

I get it, it's not always easy getting rid of things, especially if they were expensive, but holding on to them just serves as a negative reminder. Trust me when I say you are better off without them. Be resolute and decisive to really get the most out of this process. Keeping your alter ego close by can help too. What would Ava say? "You deserve better."

Onwards! You're now ready for....

Style Challenge 5

Go through the section again, critically evaluating the undecided items in each area.

Round 3

Amazing work! Don't you already feel lighter looking at your edited rail than you did when you first pulled out all your jeans? You've done really well at getting rid of all the emotional baggage and clutter in this section.

Before you put your jeans back into your wardrobe, I want you to do one last edit and sort on this section. Organise the remaining jeans/items into colours. For example, group all your blue jeans together and then within your blue jeans group the different colour-washes together e.g. your pale jeans, mid and dark blue jeans.

Then take a step back and look at where the density is. Is there an even distribution or are you top heavy in one colour? If you have more than one of each colour, identify what the difference between the same colour items are? Is it the style (skinny vs straight vs wide leg etc), the length (cropped vs long), the rise (mid, high or low). If there is enough of a point of difference between similar items, then it has earned its place in your wardrobe. Anything less and it's bye-bye darling. Place it on the appropriate discard pile.

Style Challenge 6

Arrange the remaining items into colours and style and assess for duplication.

Round 4

You should have cut the items on your rail by at least half or more. Don't panic if you've only got a few items remaining, that's totally ok, especially if they tick all the boxes in terms of flatter and fit. This is when I want you to look at what's left and identify any gaps in this section. For example, all your jeans are mid-rise, straight, medium wash. Perhaps a darker wash, same style would be a fresh injection in your wardrobe. A black pair of jeans to mix things up a bit? Or even a fresh new silhouette like the barrel style jean for example. This is your best chance to really see the wood from the tree's and identify what you need vs what you want. Start a wish-list of any items you've identified as gaps in your wardrobe to avoid falling into the mindless shopping trap again. Use the Shopping List section at the end of this book to write down any items you identify. Considered purchases are always the most sustainable and long-lasting in a wardrobe. You'll be needing this list for your shopping list which we'll be discussing in Week 12.

Style Challenge 7

Identify the gaps.

This process isn't just about creating space; it's about letting go of who you were, to make room for the bolder person you are becoming.

Round 5

Lastly, if there are any items within the final edited section that require alterations e.g. a hemline that needs taking up, shoes that need a resole. Anything that requires a fix in order for you to wear it needs to be taken out so it can be actioned. Start a 'to be mended' pile. This includes items that can be mended by you: a missing button, a bobbly jumper, an extra belt hole. If you are realistically not going to get the fix completed, consider discarding the item into one of your piles. Place the rest of the items back into your wardrobe.

Style Challenge 8

> Create an alterations pile and diarise to action.

One section down....

That may have taken you an hour or more but don't feel disheartened and overwhelmed at the task ahead. Trust me when I say it gets quicker and easier and some sections are simply bigger than others and therefore take more time. But if you follow these steps systematically, you'll end up with a streamlined wardrobe of clothes you not only love but that also flatter your shape.

Take a break, drink of water or a cup of tea and start on the next section. Repeat the process until you've gone through each section. You may prefer to tackle a section a day to spread the load and keep your mind fresh. Brain fatigue diminishes one's decision making; always declutter with a clear head. The minute you find yourself dipping or unable to make a decision, it's time to take a break or even stop for the day.

"If it doesn't fit your body or your vibe, it's time to say goodbye."

The undecideds

When it comes to dealing with the undecided items in each section, use this check-list to help your decision-making.

Does it fit?

I want you to be really honest here, by 'fit' I mean the correct size for you right now. I don't want you keeping anything in your wardrobe that's too big or too small. I'm not interested in whether you may or may not get slimmer or gain weight in the future. If, or when, that time comes, you can edit your wardrobe and shop accordingly, but right now any item that earns a place in your wardrobe needs to be the right size for you now. One of the reasons I'm so fanatical about this is because clothes that aren't the right size take up unnecessary space. They also serve as a symbol of failure, a sign you're not good enough; not slim enough or as curvy as you once were.

Either way, it's negative and this book is all about being positively BOLDER, looking and feeling fabulous and that all starts by having a wardrobe of joy, a wardrobe that's got your back, no matter how much life may be testing you right now. Think how powerful that is. It doesn't matter how bad you may feel about yourself, when you open those cupboard doors, magic awaits. Clothes that when you put them on, make you feel invincible, like you can conquer any challenge head on. That's what you're doing this for. So back to size, you get the picture, if it doesn't fit perfectly, it's a N-O.

Does it flatter your shape?

As mentioned many times in this book, clothes can enhance your curves, and hide your flaws. They are your invisibility cloak, your armour of disguise and protection from criticism. You alone have the power to look and feel good in everything you wear as long as you only have items in your wardrobe that make the most of your shape. So when you're going through the 'Round 2' edit of a section, I want you to be really discerning about the items you keep. Revisit last week for my top tips to flatter your shape. Cull anything that's a bit tight, swamps you, pulls across your bust etc. Say goodbye and move on….YES!

Does it fit into your current lifestyle?

This should be an easier question to answer, phew. Are most of the clothes in your wardrobe fit for purpose? Do they suit the lifestyle you have now or are you still holding on to a life you once had. I get it, sometimes we don't want to let go of a part of ourselves and accept the reality of where we are now. Perhaps you were a career girl but now you're a full-time mum. Or a glam city party girl and now a country casual. Life changes, good and bad, but like the size issue, there is no point holding on to clothes that serve as reminders of a life you once had. Maybe you'll go back to that one day, most likely you won't; even if you did, trust me when I say you won't be wearing those clothes again. So, let's remove any clothes that aren't fit for today's purpose. Sell them, store them (but not in your wardrobe), or donate to charity. Your call.

Does it make you feel good?

This sounds easy on paper but not always in reality. I think the simplest way to think about this is, do you like the item and is it something you can easily throw on and feel good in? For special items like a party dress it's pretty self-explanatory but for more basic items like a white t-shirt it's more of a grey area but in essence the same. Do you like the item, and do you feel confident wearing it, yes or no? And please don't hold on to something that's below par because you're waiting to find a suitable replacement. Ditch it and add a suitable replacement to your 'wish list'. You're more likely to get focused on finding a replacement if you no longer have a fall-back.

Do you wear it?

On paper, this should be pretty straightforward but just because you don't wear it, doesn't mean it's a loser. As you declutter a section you will uncover items you totally forgot about. In terms of wear regularity, if it's a total 'no' but it ticks the other boxes above it could be a 'yes'. Think about why you don't wear it before instantly relegating to the sin bin. This doesn't include things you've recently bought and haven't got round to wearing yet. I'm talking about things that for whatever reason haven't yet seen the light of day. Perhaps they just don't make you feel good when you put them on, you don't love the colour or print, they don't flatter your body shape or dare I say it those mistake buys! You may have eliminated some of these items already when you took out things that didn't fit but I'm really talking about things that sit in your wardrobe, taking up valuable space, year on year and never get a look in. It's a bit like having someone on your football team that spends the season on the bench and for whatever reason doesn't get picked for a match. Would you include them in next season's squad? Probably not.

If you're still on the fence as to whether to keep an item or not, my advice is to keep it in your wardrobe for now but make a note of what these undecided items are. Then at the end of the season if you still haven't worn it, it's unlikely you ever will. Alternatively, I put any items I'm unsure about in a box at the back of my cupboard where I can easily access them. If by the end of the season I haven't once reached into that box or given them a second thought I put them straight in the charity or resell pile. Out of sight, out of mind is usually a good test of how much you like something.

"Anything less and its bye-bye, darling."

Don't Give Up

One section down, phew! Well done on a brilliant and I hope satisfying exercise.

When you're ready, get the next section you want to edit out of your wardrobe and onto your rail. Follow the steps above systematically each time. There may be different nuances to each section e.g. dresses and blouses may also have prints, in which case follow the same process in round 5 grouping items of the same colour together but include prints within that and review for any duplicates such as too many striped shirts or floral dresses. Are they all very similar or distinctive from each other?

Once you've been through your hanging wardrobe it's time to tackle your drawers; t-shirts, knitwear, shorts etc. Declutter it all using your rail with hangers until you've streamlined every area of your closet.

It takes a lot of time to go through one's wardrobe systematically but when you're done it's a huge feeling of relief and a sense of achievement. Before you start celebrating though, there's a few more things to do:

Shoeaholics ahoy:

Do you have more shoes than clothes? Are they thrown together at the bottom of your wardrobe or packed in their own or shoe storage boxes? If you're like me, you'll be a borderline shoe-addict, which means you have more shoes then its sensible to own. Follow the same process you've done to declutter your clothes just without the rail.

Quick sweep:

Take all your shoes out of your wardrobe or storage and go through them one by one. Check for fit, comfort and condition. Anything past its best, uncomfortable or the wrong size should be relegated to the appropriate discard pile.

Out of season:

Just like our clothes, there will be some shoes that only get worn at certain times of the year. Knee high boots for example, don't tend to see the light of day in the summer months, so store them away.

Refresh:

Take out anything that needs a heel resole or a bit of love and get it sorted.

Once done put them all back in individual boxes or fit for purpose shoe storage boxes (see storage options below). Clearly label them so you know what's where and stack them at the bottom of your wardrobe, the top of your cupboard or your bespoke shoe cupboard for the lucky ones.

Style Challenge 9

> Declutter your trainers, shoes, heels and boots.

Amazing work. Have a break and some fresh air before tackling the final haul: accessories.

Pretty shiny things

Accessories are another area where we tend to accumulate lots of stuff but never review or even remember what we have. It's good to go through your accessories at least once if not twice a year to edit them down and identify any gaps.

Area's to review:

Belts:

Throw out any broken, bent or worse for wear. Do you use the others? If not, why not? Sometimes it's good to pack a few away and reintroduce the following season to mix things up and keep your wardrobe fresh. I'd suggest holding on to any belts in good condition, even if you don't use them a lot, as that may change when the real styling begins and we start creating outfits.

Jewellery:

Rings, earrings, bracelets, and necklaces. Check what you use and review anything you never wear. I wouldn't declutter your jewellery too heavily yet as you may rediscover pieces that you'd forgotten about and would work well with some of the new outfits you're going to be creating. Anything that's past its best should be relegated to the donation or charity pile but keep the 'undecided' pile close to hand for further analysis.

Scarves & hats:

Store your winter scarves/hats with your winter clothes and keep your summer scarves and hats separate. Only have seasonal items in your wardrobe at any time.

Handbags:

Handbags are collectors' items but can also accumulate and suffer from limited usage or little airtime. Go through them, see what you've got and remove anything that's past its best or out of favour. Familiarise yourself with what you have and make a point of using 2 different bags a week to mix things up. You'll be amazed at how just using a different handbag encourages you to think differently about your wardrobe and the outfits you wear.

Style Challenge 10

Declutter your accessories (bags, scarves, jewellery and belts).

The Big Tidy

As mentioned, your room is probably going to resemble the aftermath of an earthquake once you've been through everything and have various discard piles in operation. It's really important that you don't put items on these piles back into your cupboard. I see it so often; clients start off being really discerning about what to keep and what to get rid of and then never get round to properly dealing with the discard piles, the guilt sets in and it gets stuffed back into the wardrobe again.

Don't do this.

You've come so far, made such great strides to clear space in your wardrobe and free yourself from all the guilty emotions tied up in our clothes, it's important to start as you mean to go on. However, it's not always easy to throw away clothes, so here are a few suggestions on how to effectively manage the tidy up.

- **Share the love:** do you have a friend or sister you could give clothes to? It's a really positive thing to do and they may in turn have a few items for you too. Be considerate about what you give them, a huge pile of clothes that they then need to try on and sort through, isn't hugely helpful for anyone.

- **Charity pile:** I use this pile for lower value items that I'm not emotionally attached to. These need to immediately go into a bin liner and ideally the boot of your car ready for your next trip to the charity shop. Or to make the whole process even easier, book a charity collection. A lot of charities offer free collection of items. You book a slot and they will pick everything up from your front door. You could even book this in advance for a few days after your wardrobe detox to limit the chance of backtracking and rifling through the charity pile again. You've made the decision, trust yourself and let them go. Just remind yourself how much joy your items will bring someone who discovers them. It's a win-win.

- **Resell pile:** If you have items of value, you can sell them on a second-hand marketplace. It takes a bit of time to photograph and upload all the details, but you can earn quite a bit of money doing this which you can then reinvest into your wardrobe. An even bigger win-win, but it is a time commitment and you'll need to package and post any items you've sold. I would suggest only doing this for higher value items to make all the admin worthwhile. What you don't want is a pile of clothes lying around that you never get round to dealing with. That's not going to give you that liberating feeling post detox we are working towards here. Another option is to find a second clothes store near to you and sell your items through them.

- **Mend pile:** Any items that have niggling issues like a button that's fallen off or a zip that's broken or a hem that needs taking up, either deal with them yourself by allocating the time to do it or drop them off at your nearest dry cleaners for attention. It's such a good feeling removing those irritants and getting things done so you can wear your favourites again.

- **Bin pile:** This is where all the items that are not worthy of reselling, gifting or even charity go. To be more sustainable, take them to a clothes recycling depot so they can be disposed of in the right way and not end up in landfill. Especially important for man-made fibres.

It sounds like a lot but really if you're disciplined about allocating items to the right piles in the first place it's much easier to package them up and direct them to the right place after, leaving you with a lot less to tidy and a wardrobe to love. It is so easy to put all the effort into decluttering one's wardrobe and then leave clothing piles lying around for weeks on end. That's not going to make you feel any better or more importantly, bolder. See this week's challenge through right to the end to truly reap the rewards.

Style Challenge 11

Tidy up your bedroom, take anything that you're recycling to your local clothing recycling bin, bag up all your items for charity and drop them off at your local charity shop or book a free charity collection. Lastly, book a date to take any items to be altered and get it done.

Once done, take a well-deserved break before reviewing which storage solutions you need from my list below.

Stylish storage solutions

Now that you've streamlined your wardrobe you should have a lot less cluttering up the space in your closet. Am I right? That's half the battle won. The key to making the most of the clothes you've already got is being able to see it all clearly and keep it tidy (always a challenge especially when you're in a rush). Luckily, there are plenty of wardrobe organiser tools that can help. These are my recommended must-haves:

Slimline hangers:

These take up a lot less space than traditional wooden/plastic hangers. It's worth swapping all your hangers over to these to increase space in your closet.

Space saving hangers:

These are useful for hanging 3–4 pairs of jeans/trousers on one hanger, layered underneath each other.

Fabric clothes dividers:

Are brilliant for dividing up and compartmentalising your draws. Lots of options on Amazon or John Lewis. Particularly useful for your socks, bra's and pants. No more rifling through stuff to find that matching pair of socks. If you do nothing else this week, do this. It will spur you on to tackle the rest of your closet.

Stackable storage drawers:

Are fantastic for utilising shelf space and keeping your cupboard tidy. Use for knitwear, tops, t-shirts, and shorts. Anything that you usually fold and put on a shelf. Keeping them compartmentalised, helps to keep things organised and tidy. It also prevents them from getting dusty and moth-eaten too.

Shoe storage:

A few options here depending on how much space you have available. Keeping shoes in clear boxes or the boxes they came in and clearly labelled means you can stack them at the bottom of your cupboard, keeping them tidy. Alternatively or in addition, compartmentalised fabric shoe storage boxes where multiple pairs can be stored under your bed are a total winner. Another option is to display your shoes as a feature. I had shelving built in the entrance hall of my house where I display all my heels in colour order which looks great and is always a talking point at parties.

Hanging jewellery organiser:

I find this invaluable. It hangs in your cupboard or the back of your cupboard door and keeps all your necklaces, bracelets, and earrings in one place. Less scrounging, more stylish. There are lots of other jewellery organisers available, so choose one that works best for you.

Style Challenge 12

> Order the storage solutions you need. Amazon and John Lewis have everything covered.

Right, that's it for your wardrobe reinvention. I am so proud of you. I appreciate it's a lot of work and you may not be done yet, but with the right storage solutions in place, all the hard work you've invested will be easier to maintain.

Now give yourself a huge hug, pour yourself a glass of wine, no, Champagne you deserve nothing less. It's not easy letting go of things, especially when they've been a comfort blanket for so long. I totally get it, they're a big part of your identity. The thing is if you're truly going to embrace living a BOLDER life then you need to let go of things that represent the older you. No more baggy, frumpy, shapeless garb, from now on we're dialling up the style stakes.

It's time for the best part... the real styling begins.

What you will need for next week:

- **Half a day to yourself, without distractions**
- **Your clothing rail**
- **A full length mirror**
- **Your Pinterest style board (from week 2)**
- **Your mobile phone or camera**
- **A bottle of water, cup of tea or both**

THE WARDROBE EDIT

Seriously well done

on a mammoth decluttering job last week. I have no doubt there were many moments when you thought you were done, only to uncover a whole new stash of stuff you'd completely forgotten about.

Let us just take a moment to celebrate the blissful joy opening your wardrobe gives you now. That feeling of calm, satisfaction and clarity; you can now see exactly what you've got and you know that each item has a purpose, to make you look and feel good. You've also made a list of items that need an upgrade or are missing from your wardrobe, so you'll be more focused and strategic on your next shopping trip (more on that to come).

What's next?

Having a play

So, you have a detoxed wardrobe, but maybe you are not looking any bolder yet. Don't stress. This week we're going to spend some time playing in your wardrobe, the fun part. You've done the hard toil and now it's time to play dress-up. Up until now we haven't actually experimented with the clothes you've got, that starts now. We're going to be teenagers again, spending hours in front of the mirror trying on lots of outfit combinations. When I was a young girl, I would spend hours playing dress-up with my mother's clothes, sometimes even my dads, (remember the dad-cardi I told you about). Growing up in Pretoria, South Africa, there wasn't a lot of high fashion on offer, but that didn't stop me trying to create some of the looks from the *Cosmopolitan* and *My Fair Lady* magazines I'd save up to buy each month.

As we get older, our lives become driven by routines and function, so naturally there is less time to play dress-up and fantasise about the future. As such, experimenting with clothing is not something that ever crosses most people's agendas. That changes for you now. If you happen to have detoxed your wardrobe to such an extent that you have very little left to work with, feel free to skip this week and come back to it later in the process once you've invested in some new pieces for your wardrobe.

Outfit inspiration

There are lots of ways you can get outfit inspiration; Instagram, friends, magazines, observing a stylish passerby to mention a few. Where you get your fashion inspiration from doesn't matter, what's important is that you get some, as it's going to help you to create new and fresh outfits from your wardrobe.

Once you've been through this process and unlocked your true style identity, I'm positive you will become the source of your own inspiration. You may even become the aforementioned stylish passerby and end up inspiring others too. As time goes on, you'll need less external influence, as you'll have the confidence to experiment and the courage to be bolder in your style choices. The purpose of this book is to empower you to experiment freely with what you wear without getting bogged down in dos and don'ts.

This week I'm going to show you how to create outfits from what you already have and how creating a capsule will help, not in the way you expect though. Oh yes, you're never going to run out of style ideas again. Let's begin.

Firstly, let's go back to your style board and see if you're still inspired by the pictures on the RHS of your board which you selected. You're in Week 7 of this process now and you may find your style is already evolving and changing the more you tap into your wardrobe and the environment around you. You're noticing people's outfits, you're paying attention to trends, you're reading fashion magazines. It's all part of the creative process and your evolution from tired, bored dresser to being more energised and considered with everything you wear. This part of the process is all about being unconstrained and unlimited by reality in any shape or form. We're going for the dream; the more an outfit pushes you out of your comfort zone, the more you're likely to evolve in the process.

Transformation is hard on many levels. It forces you to confront how and why you're exactly where you are. How you got to this point and the potential disappointment in being somewhere you didn't want to be. But the good news is, that's the past and now we're focused on the future. The only thing that matters is the fact that you're here. You journalled lots of those feelings out in Week 2, but keep it up. It can be really cathartic to keep writing and revisiting your thoughts throughout the process.

Last week was all about clearing the negativity out of your wardrobe, those mistake buys and reminders of better days. Now you deserve some pleasure.

Outfit analysis

Before you start physically trying things on, I'd like you to take some time to review your style board again and select a couple of photos showing outfits that you'd love to wear. For each one, I'd like you to write down the building blocks of that look.

Using a blank piece of paper for each outfit, put the photo at the top and then write down what you need to create this look. For example: describe the top, trousers, blazer, shoes and other accessories. Think of it as writing down the ingredients for a recipe you want to cook for dinner. Then add a heading below for 'what you have' and another one for 'gaps'. So it looks like the example on the opposite page.

Make sure you write down all the elements and details of a look, including the shoes, bag and any other accessories such as a scarf, necklace or belt. This is important, as what will have drawn you to this outfit in the first place is the overall look, each element plays an important role. If you just pick out the core items of the look you may find it doesn't work as well. Capture the details. Learning to do this is good practice for when we come to outfit building in Week 11.

Repeat this process for each of the photos you've selected from your board ready for your try-on session. And there you have it, a selection of personalised style cards. That wasn't too difficult, was it? Next step is to convert the style cards into outfits from your existing clothes (if possible).

Building Blocks

- [ ] Purple trousers
- [ ] Floral blouse
- [ ] Pink coat
- [ ] Purple heels

Already Have

- [ ] Pink coat
- [ ] Floral blouse

Need / Gaps

- [ ] Coloured trousers
- [ ] Coloured shoes/heels

The try-on

Armed with your style cards, pick the first one and start working through your wardrobe to see which of the required building blocks for that look you already have. Hang each item on your rail and then try them all on together. Don't get too bogged down in terms of style or colour, at this point you're simply trying out a concept. If the picture features pink shoes and you only have red, that's ok. It's not about creating an exact dupe of the outfit, although that's fine too, the process is more about getting you back into the habit of experimenting with your clothes.

If the combination of elements doesn't translate in reality, swap out one of the pieces for something else. Play around, until you get an outfit that you feel confident and happy in. Take a photo of yourself in this look as a reminder and add it to your growing outfit photo bank stuck inside your cupboard door, or save it to an album in your phone if easier.

Outfit 1 – done ✓.

This is a really easy and simple way to style up new outfits. At the moment we're just using items from your existing wardrobe, but if there are specific pieces you'd really like to uplevel a look, add it to your shopping wish list.

If you've enjoyed this process you could keep going, challenge yourself to create 5–7 looks that inspire and excite you, using the same process so you have a fresh outfit for each day of the week ahead.

Taking a few hours to plan your outfits in advance takes all the headache and stress out of thinking about what to wear every morning. Spending a bit of time to curate an outfit bank will save so much stress every day. If you did this every couple of weeks, you'd quickly have 15 – 30 outfit photos you can refer to, without having to repeat an outfit too often.

Style Challenge 1

Try and create at least 2 outfits from the clothes in your wardrobe using the RHS of your style board as inspiration.

Capsule editing

Using images for style inspiration is one way to create new outfits but as you are aiming for a bold new look you may not have enough in your wardrobe to successfully be able to do this now. In which case curating a capsule wardrobe is another way of getting fresh ideas from the clothes you've already got, but it does take some creativity on your part.

The term 'capsule wardrobe' is used a lot, and it usually involves a curated selection of fairly neutral items that can easily be mixed together to create numerous outfit options. That's not the capsule I'm referring to here.

If you did some research online surrounding the so called perfect capsule wardrobe, you'll most likely get a list of very 'classic' pieces such as:

- **A white shirt**
- **A beige trench coat**
- **A black blazer**
- **Blue jeans**
- **Classic knit (grey, navy or black)**
- **Black wide leg trousers**
- **Satin blouse**
- **Neutral bodysuit**
- **Denim jacket**
- **Neutral A-line skirt**

Accessories:

- **White trainers**
- **Silver heels**
- **Black ankle boots**
- **Black tote bag**
- **Tan cross body bag**

The idea is that you then mix and match these items effortlessly together, to create numerous outfits options.

The capsule I'm referring to is also an edited number of items but the items are relevant to you and your style. Not a generic capsule that simply wipes out any individuality or self expression you may have.

Don't get me wrong, I think a capsule is a very powerful tool but whatever items you choose to include in your capsule need to represent your style, your personality.

BOLDER NOT OLDER

How to build a capsule

So let's have a go at creating a capsule. I like to think of a capsule as fluid, not stuck in stone. You don't just have one capsule in your wardrobe, you have many capsule edit possibilities. In fact, I want you to get into the habit of creating a new capsule edit from your wardrobe every 2–4 weeks.

All you do is choose a selection of clothes out of your wardrobe for your rail. Then spend half an hour mixing and matching the pieces together to create different outfit combinations. Try them on and take photos of the outfits you really like. Simple.

1 Number of items: There is no magic number when it comes to the number of pieces you should have in your capsule, however I find the ratio of 10:5 usually works. 10 items of clothing and 5 accessories.

Feel free to add more, but try to keep to 20 or under, including your accessories to make it quick and easy to create outfit combinations, otherwise, it can become a little overwhelming with too many items on your rail. As you start creating outfits, you may find you need an extra item like a blazer that would give you more outfit options. Go for it. Nothing is set in stone, if staring at a wardrobe of clothes is overwhelming, simplify by pulling out a few pieces to start with and build up from there. I find starting with a statement piece e.g. a printed dress or coloured trousers is a good starting point and add a selection of pieces that will go with these items to create different outfit options.

2 What to choose: As a starting point and to make things a little easier use the list above as a guide but tailor it to your style.

For example, instead of a white shirt you may add a leopard print blouse.

Instead of wide leg black trousers you may add slim fit black trousers.

Instead of a black blazer you include a cobalt blue blazer etc.

Just to reiterate, for the purposes of this exercise, the items in your capsule need to come from your existing wardrobe so you're making the most of what you've already got. This is about practising the art of curating an edited selection of items from your existing wardrobe to use as a foundation on which to create new fresh outfits from. This way you'll never run out of things to wear and won't fall back into the trap of same old, same old.

Let's get to it. Open that gorgeous tidy wardrobe of yours and pull out a selection of items for your rail. Don't overthink it or worry about whether you have a blazer or enough tops. Just put 10 items on your rail as a starting point and mix and match pieces together to see what outfits you can come up with. Dresses included, anything is fine, you'll quickly see what you need more or less of as you start to style things together. Go!

Style Challenge 2

Choose any 10 items and 5 accessories from your wardrobe to create your capsule.

Style Challenge 3

Mix and match items on your rail together to create some new outfit combinations and take photos for reference.

3 Mix and match: Once you've got your capsule selection hanging on your rail, start styling items together. From a good capsule you should be able to create at least 10 different outfits. Imagine how that simplifies your life? No more hassle deciding what to wear, or what goes with what, you just wear another look from your capsule and off you go.

Don't worry if you can only come up with 5 or 6 outfits, that's still fantastic, as it gives you 5 new outfit combinations to wear from what you already have.

If you're struggling for ideas, sometimes just swapping an accessory can change a look completely. For example: trainers instead of heels or a waisted belt vs no belt. Small tweaks are enough to change a look and create a new one. Don't try and change every element for each look, start with 1 look and change 1 element for the next and so on. Before you know it, you'll have 10 or more outfits to choose from. Yes, it really is that easy.

4 Capture it: Make sure you take a photo of each look and save them in your camera roll or stick inside your cupboard door for reference when you need inspiration in the morning. Once you've built up a bank of outfit photos you can use them to quickly select 5 – 7 outfits for the week ahead and put the individual elements on your rail ready for easy access. That's effortless dressing at its best. You're welcome.

Why bother?

Make the most of what you have:

Well, the main reason a capsule is useful is because you make the most of what you have. It gives you many outfit options out of a small selection of clothes, meaning you'll get more wear out of your wardrobe. As I've shown in the outfit pictures above, once you select your items you can easily mix and match them together to create new combinations.

Now imagine how much more use you would get out of your existing clothes, if you created a new capsule for yourself every two weeks. This is honestly one of the best ways to be sustainable and shop less; creating new outfit combinations from what you already have. And that doesn't mean you have to create 7 new outfits each week, just switching a blouse or changing your shoes can alter the vibe of an outfit. You don't have to reinvent the wheel all the time.

Save time:

A capsule approach instantly reduces daily overwhelm as you have less items to choose from overall. Planning in advance means getting dressed every day is as easy as 1, 2, 3. With no stress or fuss, looking good becomes the standard.

Save money:

Instead of constantly shopping for a new outfit, you'll be creating new looks out of your existing wardrobe. When you do invest in something new, it's with purpose, not just for the sake of 'newness'.

Strategic shopping:

When I do a seasonal shop with my clients, I always prepare an edited capsule for them ensuring anything they buy can be mixed and matched together and integrate seamlessly with what they already have.

BOLDER NOT OLDER

Avoid outfit fatigue:

Coming up with new outfit combinations everyday can quickly lead to fatigue and cycling back to comfort. Having an edited capsule, which you rotate every few weeks will prevent you getting bored and falling back into your old habits and comfort zone. We shouldn't ignore everything else we have in our wardrobes either, which is why I suggest rotating your capsule every few weeks to keep it fresh and ensure getting dressed is fun.

Lots of creativity this week! I hope you're enjoying playing dress-up with your wardrobe. How many outfits did you manage to create from your first capsule edit? And how many style cards did you manage to recreate? I hope it's been fun and you're enjoying styling yourself in new and different ways.

Next week, we're going to paint the town red, so savour the calm before the colour explosion ahead.

ALL THINGS BOLD & BRIGHT

It's impossible to have a bad day in a bright outfit!

Ladies, you've built the foundation from the ground up and now it's time to turn up the heat and really get BOLD. No wallflowers are welcome here. From now on we're stepping out of our shells, throwing our comfort zone out with the bath water and giving ourselves permission to let our hair down, stop caring what anyone else thinks and be BOLD.

WEEK 8

This is Week 8, you're well over halfway through this process and it's time to take your transformation to new heights. After all, that is why you're here, right?

Colour is the number one thing that consistently surprises and delights my clients when it comes to their personal style, it's why most of my clients come to me in the first place, knowing they want to wear more colour, but either don't know how or don't have the confidence to do it.

Not only that, there are literally millions of colours that have now been created, that sheer amount of diversity and choice in clothing every season leads to total overwhelm and confusion. This results in many women sticking with so-called 'safe' colours such as black, grey and navy. While these neutrals can certainly form part of your wardrobe and do look wonderful in some instances, they can also lack the personality and energy of brighter colours. One thing they most certainly will not do is make you feel BOLD and more importantly visible.

Dressed in colour will help you to radiate from the inside out in a way that isn't possible with neutrals. Colours have such an enormous power over how we look and feel. As well as affecting the aesthetics of your Image, they also positively impact on your mood and the energy you exude. You can use colour to help you stand out in a crowd, create a lasting and memorable impression and above all display vitality and vibrance. Colour is the key ingredient if you really want to step into your power during your mid-life and feel 'Bolder not Older'.

Neon dreams

Are you ready to be bold and turn on the rainbow in your wardrobe? I'm hoping that even if you're a little nervous about colour and wearing it, you're open to the idea of exploring it to see if you can be convinced?

Don't worry, you're not going to have to dress in neon head to toe, but as much as an all-neutral outfit can look sophisticated and elegant, it's simply not going to make you stand out. To truly embrace your boldness, to show the world just how fabulous you really are and most importantly, to help you to feel visible again, the best way to do this is with colour.

It's time to get your glow-torch out girl and shine.

> "Colour isn't just what you wear—it's how you dare."

What you need

Colour is such a big topic that many people have written whole books just focusing on it. If you know me by now, I like to uncomplicate things as much as possible, as then you're more likely to embrace the advice.

So for this weeks challenges, I want to take you on a journey. I hope that by the end of it, you'll be shocked to see, not only how far you've come but also how easy it was. From experience, I know that if I just hold up a bright red blouse and tell you to wear it, you won't. If, instead, I style you in an outfit that's well put together and happens to include a red blouse, you will most likely love it.

It's not about the colour, it's the outfit that counts.

My advice is to read through this whole chapter first, taking notes of the tasks that I've devised for you, before deep diving into your wardrobe to pull items that would be suitable for each challenge.

Just as you've been doing for your wardrobe edit exercises, but this time colour is going to be the central theme of your selection. Doing this will also help you identify any pieces you don't have and that's ok. I will talk you through what to do about that, as we move through the process.

One last thing, for the purpose of these style challenges, it's easier to work with separates than dresses, but don't panic if you have a wardrobe full of dresses. Use layers like a jacket or accessories to create the same effect.

Think outside of the box, don't give up just because an item doesn't come to mind at first. A statement ring, a coloured pair of socks or shoes can add contrast too. Use what you have as a starting point, you'll be amazed at what you can create from what you already have.

> "It's not about the colour, it's the outfit that counts."

Colour basics

Before we get into the styling bit let's just get some terminology out of the way so we're all on the same page. As mentioned there are 1000s of colour variations out there, but I don't want to get too technical, as that will detract from the creativity I want to inspire in this chapter. I don't want you to overthink colour or worry too much about getting it perfect, I just want you to experiment and have fun. The purpose of this 12 week transformation programme is to open your eyes to the power of colour and show you how to incorporate it into your wardrobe, creating impactful outfits that make you feel bold and visible. However I appreciate this can feel daunting, so here are my top tips, without getting too technical, about how to determine if a colour suits you are not.

1 Face first: It may seem self-explanatory, but you only need to worry about suitability when it comes to colour worn right up against your face, through tops, scarves, or jewellery; anywhere else on the body simply doesn't count. For instance, mustard is not a colour that flatters my complexion but that doesn't mean I can't wear it. A mustard skirt or trousers would look great teamed with teal on top, it's on the opposite end of the colour wheel, and a more flattering colour for my skin tone. It also looks great as an accessory, belt, socks, shoes, or bag etc.

2 First sight: A quick and easy way to check if a colour suits you is to hold it up against your face or better, put it on. Then close your eyes for a few seconds and open them up. What do you notice first? The colour or your face? If all you see is the item, it's dominating you and draining the colour out of your face. If you notice your face first, the colour will be infusing your complexion, your skin will look healthy and your eyes will sparkle. If it's not a good fit, your skin will look washed out and sallow, dark circles will be more noticeable.

3 Skin tone: Do you have a cool or warm complexion? As a most simple explanation, cooler complexions tend to be paler in nature and warmer complexions tend to be darker. Try wearing something orange vs pink. If you look better in the orange, you're warm, if pink, you're most likely to be cool.

Another trick is to look at the veins on your wrist or palm. If your veins appear green, you have a warm complexion. Blue or purple veins means you have a cool complexion. And if you have a mix or you can't tell, you are more likely to be neutral which means you can probably wear most colours.

I have a cool complexion, but I tend to wear any colour I like and just adapt my make-up if my skin needs an extra boost. The only colours I tend to avoid wearing right up against my face are what I call dirty colour tones for a better word to describe them, the burnt oranges, mustards, khaki greens etc. Mediterranean colours that look fabulous on darker, warmer skin tones but wash out a pale complexion. But that doesn't stop me from wearing them on my lower half or as accessories.

If you're warm

Go to colours:

Rust, peach, gold, orange, turquoise, moss green, yellow, warm red (tends towards orange).

Neutrals:

Dark brown, navy, olive, camel, cream, ivory.

Hard to wear colours:

Cool, icy colours such as pale blue and jewel tones such as ruby red, purple, emerald green and fuschia pink.

Jewellery:

Gold, copper or bronze, warm stones and enamels.

If you're cool

Go to colours:

Plum, lavender, rose pink, fuchsia, royal or bright blue, emerald, burgundy, blue reds.

Neutrals:

Black, grey, navy, white, soft white

Hard to wear colours:

Oranges and yellows, warm or golden colours.

Jewellery:

Silver, platinum, cool stones, pearl and enamels.

4 Just go for it: Many women I meet are so fearful when it comes to experimenting with colour in case they get it wrong, they play it safe and never dare to go bold. Yes it's true some colour hues will suit you better than others, but honestly for the purposes of this 12 week process I want you to throw caution to the wind and just go for it. What have you really got to lose?!

Remember this is meant for guidance only. Don't get stuck in a rut of 'I can only wear certain colours'. Being bolder is about freedom, risk and liberty, not rules, regulation and worrying about getting it 'right'.

Colour categories

As you work your way through this week's style challenges you'll see I've grouped colours into categories to make them easier to refer to. Here's a breakdown of what these are:

Classic neutrals:

I classify a neutral as black, white, grey or cream.

Interesting neutrals:

Darker colours like navy, brown, forest green, khaki maroon, burgundy and denim are also great options for layering a colour pop against. More interesting than a classic neutral and often a softer canvas to mix colours with. If wearing too much colour isn't for you, I would highly encourage you to invest in darker neutrals to layer up with, as black and white can both drain the colour they are paired with.

Pastels:

Softer shades of colour, think ice-cream shades, pale pink, lilac, pale blue, mint green, lemon yellow, peach. You get the picture. Softer in hue but still colourful and a great alternative to bold brights. Pastels are also a good way to ease yourself into wearing more colour, especially in the summer months.

Brights:

I think of brights as the richest hue of a colour, a real standout: cobalt blue, emerald green, sunshine yellow, orange, fuchsia, red or purple. The true colour pops that you can spot a mile away.

That's all you need to know for now. In terms of how to know if a colour suits you or not, I don't want you to worry about that too much. We're mostly playing with clothes you already have in your wardrobe, and I don't want you to overthink anything, just go for it and have fun. If all else fails just add lipstick! I am slowly but surely going to get you to a place where wearing colour is something you not only embrace but fall in love with.

Off to the red carpet or the yellow brick road we go… you choose!

WEEK 8

Let the colour challenges begin!

Let's start at the beginning, a safe place. I'm hoping you already have some colour in your wardrobe, likely not enough, but a good place to make a start. You've done the hard work and organised your wardrobe so you should be able to clearly see the colour you already have to work with. Below are some colour concepts I'd like you to experiment with starting at the top.

1 **Colour + neutral:** I want you to pick out your brightest colour, ideally a block colour rather than a print. Preferably trousers, or a blouse. I'd like you to style this with a classic neutral and wear it tomorrow, whatever you're doing – wear it all day long.

In your journal write down any comments you receive and also take note of how you felt wearing it. The more we observe our thoughts and emotions, the clearer and more in tune we become when something really feels good (or not). Life is so busy, most of the time we don't even have awareness of why we're not feeling great. Today is a big change, you're putting yourself out there and going bold, take note of how it feels.

Style Challenge 1

Style a colourful item with a neutral and wear it outside the house. Take photos to remind you of this look.

2 **Colour + interesting neutral:** Can I just say how amazing you are. You haven't given up on me, the book, this process and most importantly yourself. I can tell how invested you are in your transformation and determined to cross the bridge to BOLD leaving AVERAGE behind for good.

Yesterday wasn't so bad was it? Such a simple thing to do and how many compliments did you get?

Still feel invisible? I'm hoping it was a positive experience and now you're hungry for more.

Today we are going to dial things up a notch and instead of blending a block colour with a classic neutral, I want you to try and style it with a more interesting neutral, but not blue jeans, as we all know you can wear denim with practically anything. Navy trousers and a fuschia pink blouse or khaki cargo's with an orange t-shirt? Again, nothing too complicated, just elevating things a notch. Notice how the bright looks softer against the more interesting neutral. Now compare it against black or white. Can you see what I mean? Black and white are extremes on the colour spectrum, devoid of colour themselves, they can draw the life blood out of even the boldest of palettes, so it's good to experiment with other neutrals to add interest to your wardrobe. Again, observe any compliments you receive and how you feel in this outfit.

Don't worry if it doesn't resonate as well as some of the others in this challenge, it's all about finding your colour centre, the level of colour you feel most happy with. It may be outside of your comfort zone of course.

Style Challenge 2

> Style a colourful item with an interesting neutral and wear it to work or to whatever you are doing today. Any feedback?

3 **Tonal colours:** Today we are going to liven things up a tiny bit, don't worry. I want you to create a tonal look or at least try to, created from the clothes you already have. What I mean by tonal is the same colourway top to toe, with different intensities mixed together. Try mixing a bold bright with an interesting neutral, as you did yesterday, only this time they have to be from the same colour family e.g. green. You could team emerald green with forest green, bright red with burgundy, maroon with a bold purple or even teal with navy. Remember, one colour family, different intensities.

If you're someone who feels more comfortable in neutrals this is an extension of that, cream and white together, grey and black. It's a great way to use colour for impact without it being in-your-face, so to speak. Give it a try and observe how it feels and how others react to you. Which outfit so far has got the most attention? As we're aiming for visibility it's good to consider which outfit combinations are working for you.

Don't stress if you don't have anything suitable, instead perhaps use the day's challenge to research some items to buy that you could style together for this challenge to add to your wish list and try it on another day. Or go into a shop and experiment with this concept in the changing room.

Style Challenge 3

> Style two colours from the same colour spectrum but in different tones together.

Simplicity is the ultimate sophistication, and a tonal outfit speaks that fluently, layering shades of the same hue to create elegance without excess.

4 Colour blocking: All good? I am so utterly proud of you and your fearlessness with the way you've tackled this week's challenges. I can feel the energy reverberating off you, the colour magic is working.

Today we are going to leave the neutrals completely behind and work on a colour block.

What is a colour block?

A colour block is when you style two colours together, technically any two colours of a completely different colour tone for example green and pink. So, here's a surprise, you've already been doing it with the first two challenges this week, except one of the colours was a neutral shade. Today we are going to experiment with styling two contrasting colours together known as a colour block. The intensity of these colours is entirely up to you. You could style two pastel tones together or turn up the heat with two brights styled together. Or mix a pastel and a bright for example mint green and fuchsia pink. The options are endless, you can really have fun with this. Try not to overthink it too much or worry about what colours go with what, just go for it. If it starts to feel too much, scale it back and take the pressure off yourself. You're almost there, and if this is your limit right now, that's absolutely fine. You've still worn more colour in a week than you've probably done in a lifetime which is amazing. I hope you're buzzing either way.

As a stylist I have to work within a client's boundaries all the time, knowing when I can push someone over the line and when its best to hold back and ease them slowly over a few sessions is what makes me good at what I do. Even if I know something is going to look amazing on a client, it won't get worn if they don't believe it too. I want to help you to flick that switch when you're ready to. Great style is a process of evolution, big changes simply don't happen overnight. Take your time, breathe and go easy on yourself. The transformation is happening, whether you finish this task today, tomorrow or a few weeks' time, nothing is lost, as long as you stay invested.

Which colours to choose

I don't want to be prescriptive but if you're someone who needs clear guidance about which colours to mix together, have a look at the colour wheel (next page). Colours that sit opposite each other on a colour wheel are complementary colours and will create a beautiful clash.

Now go to your wardrobe and see if you have any colours you can block together and try them on. Eek too bright? You know what, it is bright, but never too much. Take yourself, your head and your emotions out of it and critically evaluate the combination as if someone else was wearing it. What would you think seeing this outfit on someone else? Would you admire it? Would you wish it was something you could pull off? In which case, hear me when I say this. You can.

And you will. All you have to do is wear it. Forget about the colour boldness and just get on with your day as normal. Avoid all mirrors if it's easier, I just want you to wear the outfit outside of the house!

Even if it's just around the block, the grocery store or on the school run. Get it out there. It won't be as bad as you think, in fact it's going to feel amazing. And remember, if you can't find anything in your wardrobe that would work, use accessories to create the block. A bright red bag against a pink blouse for example. Observe and journal at the end of the day.

Style Challenge 4

Style any two colours together as long as one of them isn't a neutral or interesting neutral. This is your chance to start wearing colour top and bottom. No hiding!

5 Head to toe: For your final colour challenge, I want you to create an outfit in the same colour head to toe. Pick any colour you like, a lot will depend on what you have available, but it has to be the same colour top and bottom. Ideally not a classic neutral, but anything from any of the other colour groups we've worked through this week is fine. It doesn't have to be bright. I just want you to get the feeling of wearing one colour top to toe. The other thing to note is when you wear a bright red blouse with jeans for example, the focal point of the outfit will definitely be the blouse. But when you wear a red blouse with red trousers, the focal point is the outfit overall, not the colour or the blouse particularly, just the look. It's a brilliant way to draw attention to and away from yourself i.e. be noticed because of your outfit but not your size, shape or age.

I'm inherently quite shy, I always have been. I love an audience but don't ask me to walk into a room of unknowns and make small talk. It's literally my worst nightmare. Like it or not though, some things just must be done. So when I'm faced with an evening of chit chatting with people I don't know, I always wear one colour top to toe. I know I'm guaranteed to stand out and be noticed. That way people gravitate towards me and the colour I'm wearing, they start talking to me, which makes it far easier for me to chat to them in return. Red is my favourite colour to style, top to bottom. It always makes me feel like a million dollars, even if the pieces in themselves are quite classic, the colour does all the talking for me.

When it comes to surviving your biggest challenges in life, your clothes are your secret weapon. Colour is the secret ingredient that helps you to stand out, whatever your size or age, it always works.

Style Challenge 5

> Style one colour head to toe, no neutrals please! I said choose any colour for this task but actually I'd secretly love it if you wore a bright, bold colour head to toe. I know you're ready. You can do this.

Hooray, you've made it to the end of the week. Wow, you have certainly painted the town bright. I hope by now it feels less daunting, more enjoyable and you're starting to appreciate how empowering colour can be. You're no longer invisible or unnoticed. You've got a glow back in your skin and a spring in your step.

Who knew colour was the secret ingredient to feeling younger? Well I did actually, and now you do too.

Moral of the story: If you're open to wearing more colour, you can and you will. You just have to be willing to try and go for it. Remember what's the worst that can happen? Will the earth still be spinning when you get home? I think so.

I hope you've had fun this week, you should certainly be feeling bolder and brighter; just when you thought the hard bit was done, next week gets even more fruity.

THE PRINT EFFECT

Oh wow, wow, wow.

I can feel the energy and excitement reverberating from your pores. Last week was a big week. I know, you may feel a bit angry and frustrated at yourself for being so reticent about wearing colour for so long; worried about what people would say or think. Now that the canary is out of her cage, her wings will never be clipped again, am I right? Are you starting to become a closer version of your alter ego by now?

How to style colour is one of the most powerful skills a woman can learn. It will never fail you or let you down, meaning you will always look and feel better about yourself, your age and your life whenever you wear and embrace it.

But just when you thought you'd conquered the tip of the style challenges, there is more to come. This week we're going to expand your styling skills that bit further and immerse ourselves in all things print. This is where you add personality to your wardrobe. Some of you may feel delighted, others less so, but you know there's no easy way through this, the road to BOLD is direct and unwavering in its purpose. You've already broken down so many barriers, I think you'll find this week's challenges won't drive you dotty.

The subtle art of diversion

I've often mentioned throughout this book how an inordinate amount of time and energy gets invested in covering up areas of our body we don't like. The bits we feel most self-conscious about get most of our attention. Usually resulting in a compromised outfit, as the focus is on concealment rather than creating a stylish look. The failsafe solution usually being to opt for darker colours or neutrals, alongside lots of volume to cover our perceived imperfections. But there is another way, a far more effective toolkit to achieve the same thing whilst not compromising the quality, shape or fit of your outfit and that's by wearing print.

What's in a print

In the same way a colour can work to draw your eye to an area of your body when worn with a darker or lighter contrasting colour tone – think of the first colour challenge we did last week – so will a print. In fact, if wearing block colours still doesn't sit comfortably with you, print could be your new best friend. The beauty of a print is that to the viewer, all you see is the print.

No 'wobbly bits', 'fat rolls', 'dimpled' or 'saggy skin' or in fact any other imperfection you want to hide. Zilch. A bit like a magic eraser marker that sits in your wardrobe. Print is THE master of disguise, and although we're not in the business of hiding, we are in the business of flaunting our assets to perfection and print is a powerful tool to help you achieve that.

Here's a little exercise to test this theory, you may need to go into a store to do this if you don't have the right pieces to hand in your wardrobe. Pop out for 10 minutes in your lunch break or while the kids are at school; it's an important one, so you won't want to miss doing this.

For this week's first challenge, I want you to compare wearing a bold colour to a print, on the part of your body you're most self conscious about. So if you're not a fan of your tummy then try a dress or blouse and if it's your hips then a dress, trousers or a skirt will work. All I want you to do is to pick an item and try it on in a bold colour and then in a bold print. Take a photo of each and observe which item/outfit you look/feel slimmer in. I can 100%

guarantee that any lumps and bumps will be less visible in the print. Colour is wonderful but can be less forgiving depending on the fabric and fit. Whereas a print will never let you down irrespective of the style or fabric.

Style Challenge 1

Test wearing a bold colour vs a printed item on the part of your body you like the least. What happens?

Print phobia

When I ask my clients what their pet hates are, one of the common answers is wearing print. But print is such a broad term, it's like saying I never wear colour, and I know in 99% of situations that's simply not true. Unless of course, you only ever wear neutrals head to toe, which most people don't.

In fact, when I drill down with my clients as to whether it's ALL print or certain prints that are the issues, floral prints usually come out tops. Often irking back to a childhood experience, or just how wearing a floral print makes some people feel. I totally get it, I certainly don't like all manner of floral prints. But there's floral and floral – no two florals are the same. I personally prefer bigger, bolder florals (no surprises there) than a small ditsy one. The smaller floral prints like the *Laura Ashley* or *Liberty Print* variety just make me feel frumpy. No logic. It's just a personal thing. Some prints will feel like you, others won't.

One of my favourite things to do is challenge my clients' perceptions, especially when it comes to print. If they say they can't do floral, I will go out of my way to find a floral that works. Not just to prove a point, but to show them that we should never write something off as a headline. Always give it a try, you may surprise yourself when you see something on. It's important to assess an item when it's part of an outfit and not in isolation, as it can totally change how you feel in it.

Stripes, dots and other creatures

Print is such a wide and diverse category. When you stop to think about just how many different types and styles of prints there are, the options are endless. Whether you're a fan or foe, there is most definitely a print out there for you, it's just a matter of finding it. Let's take a look at some of the options:

1. **Stripes:** Possibly one of the most timeless, iconic prints in the world, especially in the summer season. Think *Breton* stripes, multi striped dresses and striped accessories like scarves. There is literally no one who can't wear a stripe.

There is literally no one who can't wear a stripe.

How to stripe…

There is logic to the direction of stripe you use; if you're looking to slim and elongate proportions, a vertical stripe is your best friend. Alternatively wearing a horizontal stripe on your top half if you're smaller chested will add breadth and help balance the hips.

However, don't feel you need to restrict yourself to this. The width of the stripe will naturally create more of an effect. In other words, if you love the idea of wearing a *Breton* stripe but have a large bust, there's no reason why you couldn't as it's a thin stripe and its broadening properties will therefore be less. Look for tops with a wider neckline or even a v-shape to further flatter the bust. Another trick is to layer a slim horizontal stripe under a blazer; a good look for any shape to be honest, but for large busts, the blazer lapel will create a plunging V-shape to offset the width of the stripe.

To really up the style stakes, look for a medium width stripe, either two tone or multi-coloured for real pizazz. A multi-coloured vertical stripe is a wonderful choice for a dress. Effortless yet impactful. Add it to your wish list and keep your eye out for one, I promise it will be worth the wait. I've got a striped suit (not pin-stripe, much bolder than that) on my want list, I have yet to find the right one, but I know it's out there.

2 Spots: Who doesn't love a dotty print? Spot's are another popular print which are pretty safe and hard to get wrong, but always eye-catching just the same.

How to spot the right dot

Like stripes, there are many variations of the spot. Monochrome being the obvious and most popular choice but also look out for coloured spots or white spots on a coloured background. As with stripes, consider the placement and size of the spots when choosing this print. If you're after concealment, then the bigger the dots the better. A small spotty print won't do much in the camouflage stakes, you need to go bigger on this one. The great thing about dots is that as an asymmetric print it maximises the potential for disguise, as the eye can't focus on one area. My advice is don't be held back too much on size, but if you're worried about drawing attention to the wrong area, then opting for a dress where the print is consistent will be more flattering.

3 Check: I consider check a symmetric print, yet the busy nature of it makes it eye catching as well as flattering. There are plenty of variations to choose from, but the most common in the fashion stakes are dog tooth, tartan, gingham and a classic chequerboard style print.

Check mate

When choosing a check print, a lot is down to personal preferences. Not everyone likes gingham, and while some love tartan, others can't stand it. I think it is definitely a print worth exploring. Small and medium sized checks work well on tops and trousers, tartan for skirts and accessories and dog tooth for coats. That's a broad generalisation so, as always, please don't limit yourself

to these options. Choose the size of the print based on the level of camouflage or distraction you're going for or go all out with a check print head to toe like I have on the cover of this book. Any size of check can be a winner in the style stakes.

If you're worried about how to style an outfit around a check print, it's probably easier to go for a monochrome print, then you can put any colour or neutral with it, whilst still creating a show-stopping look. If you choose a gingham style print with one colour and white, then style it with a matching block colour to complement.

4 Animal: Probably the most universal of prints and worn by all. I have yet to meet anyone who doesn't love a spot of leopard. In fact, it's usually something I'd advocate as a strong addition to a client's wardrobe, it's such a versatile print that never disappoints. It's usually always available on the high street too, so it's easy to find if you want to try it. And no, you're definitely not too old to wear it!

What's your spirit animal?

Leopard is the most popular and common of all the animal prints, followed by snake, zebra and tiger prints. Mostly found in neutral colour combinations, meaning you can style it as a neutral base and block it against a bright. My all-time favourite is leopard print worn with a bold red or even fuchsia pink; it never lets me down when I want to make a statement. Animal prints are also asymmetric in nature which increases their disguise-rating.

Choose your animal according to what's available or your preference.

Growing up in South Africa, I had many trips to the game reserve for holidays where large snakes were often hiding in the roof beams or on a tree. Can't say it made me feel comfortable knowing they were there; as a result, I can't wear anything with a snake print. It's a bit too close to home for me. Sometimes we just have personal reasons for not being able to wear something, and that's totally ok, as long as it doesn't hold you back from experimenting with other prints.

It's also fun to look out for an animal print in a bold colour combination for something different. Style with a neutral or block colour to complement. Equally if you already have some leopard in your wardrobe, branch out and invest in another animal print to add to your collection.

If you're not a big print fan, then I'd go as far to say a classic leopard print is a good place to start. It's pretty safe, and hard to get wrong, making it one of the easiest prints to wear. Try it and see how it feels.

5 Florals: In spring summer, floral prints are in abundance. It's hard to get away from them to be honest, but that's not necessarily a bad thing.

How to be a bloomer

As mentioned previously, florals can invoke a love/hate response. Unlike animal print which is hard to get wrong, florals can easily be hit and miss. One bad experience and it's unlikely you'll ever want to go back. If you're a floral lover then great, you will almost certainly have a floral print that you gravitate towards. If you're a bit of a wallflower though, then my advice is to go....unsurprisingly...for a bolder floral print, and make a statement with it.

Avoid the small, ditsy, country style floral prints as these can miss the mark and make you feel older rather than bolder as it's harder to get the balance right. Whereas a stronger, bigger floral print is much easier to wear. Less English country garden and more designer flower arrangement. Look to designers like *Dolce & Gabbana*, who I always think design floral prints so well, striking the right balance between feminine whilst still being statement.

6 Geometric: Prints that feature a repetitive shape in a uniform nature, that don't fit into one of the categories above, are often referred to as geometric. Often striking and a good option for the floral foe, especially if you're not ultra girly, but like the idea of incorporating more print into your wardrobe. Follow the same principles already mentioned above. The only thing to consider is the size and closeness of the print; too small and symmetric, you could end up looking like a curtain. Once again, bigger is bolder and of course...better.

7 Motif prints: We often see a motif print being a seasonal trend on the catwalk. These prints can feature fruits (e.g. oranges and lemons), actual animals (e.g. dogs and horses) and other symbols such as stars, hearts, lips, chains and bows. Motifs can really add a touch of personality to your wardrobe. They have the ability to make you feel cheerful when you wear them. One of the main ingredients of feeling BOLD is being happy. They also tend to be more unusual than some of the more mainstream prints mentioned above, so a good way to add that unique edge to your wardrobe. Dare I say it, they are always a great conversation point. Whenever I wear my lips blouse someone will always comment on it – in a good way of course. It's probably not something I would advocate wearing top to toe and is best suited to a top or blouse in most instances.

So there we have it, I think that covers off most print styles that you'll find on the high street, have a closer look at your newly decluttered wardrobe and identify what prints you currently have, put them on your rail and then let's take a deep dive into how to style your prints, to create amazing outfits.

Print Tactics

Before I get onto the nitty gritty, a few top line things to think about.

All over vs one element

I touched on this briefly above, but just to make the point again in case you missed it. If you're worried about breaking up the body and drawing attention in the wrong direction, then I would advocate an all-over consistent print either as a dress, co-ord or even a suit. Gosh, a suit? Definitely not for the faint hearted but actually very effective and a total showstopper, if you can find the right one. Ava's often wearing a statement printed suit, go Ava!

An all over print will completely melt any imperfections away, all you'll see is the print. It will also hide sweat marks and creases which can help the confidence stakes for important meetings or events when you want to feel relaxed and look your best.

Large vs small

The bigger and bolder the print the more of a statement it will create. Choose the size of print according to the tone of the event you're going to. If it's a more formal occasion than a smaller print will be a better choice. A party or wedding and a bright, bold, large print will bring the right spirit.

Monochrome vs colour vs neutrals.

Just as above, tailor your colour choice of print to the occasion. Monochrome prints, especially if worn all over, will be the most eye-catching, making an entrance when you walk in.

Next up will be a colourful print, definitely less formal in nature but so few of us have a 'formal' existence these days, and just the nature of wearing a print will separate you from most people. Neutral prints such as animal prints, are the most versatile and unless worn head to toe relatively understated in my book, although you may not feel that way if you're a print virgin. I get it, but don't let that hold you back from giving it a try.

How to style print

Whatever your original view of wearing print was, I hope reading through this chapter so far has sparked a little curiosity as to whether it's something you could embrace in your wardrobe. I'd really like you to try.

Small steps as always, and before you know it, you'll be head-to-toe in a print clash. Well perhaps not, but let's keep our minds open to all possibilities to see where your creativity leads you on this week's style exploration.

1 **As is:** I'm going to be really nice and ease you into wearing print. Today's challenge, if you choose to accept it, is to pull any printed item out of your wardrobe, yes any, and wear it. Doesn't matter what it is or how you style it, just wear it. That's a great start. As always take a moment to observe yourself in the mirror, how do you look and how does it feel wearing this print?

Style Challenge 2

Wear a print today, anything with a print.

2 **To complement:** Fabulous, that wasn't too bad, was it? Today we're going to raise the bar slightly. What I want you to do is take the same print or another print, your choice, and style it with an item or accessory that matches one of the colours in the print. It doesn't matter whether it's a neutral or a bold colour, just take a look at the colours in the print and see what you have available that will match to the print. If a dress is your outfit of choice, then add a blazer or an accessory such as a belt or shoes that complement one of the colours in the print.

Style Challenge 3

Pick out one or even two of the colours in the print and choose an item(s) to add to your outfit.

3 **To contrast:** This works best for neutral prints like a monochrome or animal print where the colours have a classic neutral base. Instead of styling the print with items that complement or match, throw in an unexpected pop of colour instead. The bolder the better. This is an easy way to inject real personality into an outfit. For example, a splash of neon will give any outfit a fashion twist.

Style Challenge 4

Add a pop of colour to a neutral print with accessories.

Phew. What a chapter that was. I hope you enjoyed indulging the playful side of your style this week in all things print. Print is so much fun to wear and it adds a fresh dimension to a wardrobe, with the added bonus of disguising anything you don't want an observer to notice. A miracle suit in the making, right there in your wardrobe! If print is a big gap in your closet, it's worth adding a few pieces to your wish list and revisiting this chapter when they arrive.

Nine weeks down, three to go, almost there. What more could there possibly be to talk about? Just you wait, the best is still to come!

> "Wearing prints is like speaking without words—it's bold, playful, and unapologetically you."

BLING IT ON

week 10

Accessories are the magic wands that can transform an outfit from mundane to magnificent.

The unsung heroes of fashion, the cherry on top, the sparkle that brings your entire outfit together. From statement necklaces to classic bracelets, chic scarves to elegant hats, the right accessory can elevate your style, express your personality, and make a powerful statement.

In this chapter, we are going to delve into an area of style most close to my heart: the art of accessorising. You'll discover how to choose the perfect pieces to complement your wardrobe, learn the secrets to layering and combining different accessories and understand how to balance bold and subtle items to create harmony in your outfits. Whether you're dressing for a casual day out, a professional setting or a glamorous evening event, the right accessories can enhance your look and boost your confidence.

Get ready to explore the transformative power of accessories and learn how to use them to express your unique style.

The finishing touches

Accessories make-eth the outfit. They are what separates the uber stylish from everyday style. Get it right, you'll be walking out a showstopper, wrong and you'll resemble a Christmas tree. So, what are the options and how many accessories do we need?

According to celebrity stylist Rachel Zoe 'Accessories are more important than clothes', in other words we should be spending more of our shopping budget on accessories than seasonal trend items. The great thing about accessories is that they have more longevity than clothes.

You don't need to rush out and buy a load all at once, think of them more as building a collection archive over time. In my experience women usually have a lot of clothes but not a wide selection of accessories. If this is proving to be a gap in your wardrobe, which for most of my clients it is, don't panic. Make a point of investing in a few new accessory pieces each season and slowly build it up. Good accessories will last a lifetime, the aim is to start slowly and build up, as your confidence in accessorising grows.

Be mindful, a lot of ladies have their go-to accessories, be it bracelets, a necklace or earrings that are worn on repeat, day-in, day out. That my friend, is not what I mean by accessorising at all!

High street vs designer

The right accessories can make a cheap outfit look expensive. They can pull an outfit together, create a focal point or simply inject a bit of style into an otherwise unremarkable look. Accessories are all about adorning an outfit to make it look special and add your personal flair. They can also be used to make a strong statement about your own or aspiring financial status, your style signature or to simply inject colour and personality into an outfit.

The secret is not in the price point but in finding accessories you absolutely love and can't live without. There is nothing nicer than having a few coveted designer or high end pieces from brands you really admire, but most of my standout accessory pieces come from the high street.

Things to consider when purchasing accessories are:

Budget

Whether you opt for high end or high street depends on your budget, but also consider the pound per wear of an item. Is it a one-off piece or something that you will use again and again? A statement belt will stand you in good stead for decades, and is often well worth the extra price tag if it's something you can wear with most outfits. High end accessories will last better than high street ones. So a classic black designer belt with a statement gold buckle for example is something you can add to most outfits which will weather the storm of your wardrobe for much longer than a cheaper high street alternative. It will also add that extra glam factor to a cheaper outfit. Consider how much you're likely to use and wear an accessory when making an investment purchase. It could turn out to be better value than a high street alternative that falls apart after a season and more sustainable too. But the high street is a good place to start if you're new to accessorising and want to experiment with different options.

Colour

There is a tendency to invest in neutral accessories as they will be more versatile; and although it's good to have accessories in neutral tones that you can add to any outfit, the real wow factor unsurprisingly, is with bolder coloured accessories. A red belt instead of a black belt or a pair of neon yellow shoes to pair with a navy outfit. In fact, if wearing lots of colour is still something you're not 100% on board with then this is a less intimidating, easy and striking way to uplevel your outfit. Most of my clients have a selection of neutral accessories (belts, shoes, bags etc); you've probably got a black version, possibly a tan version, perhaps something in cream? Now I want you to focus on investing in colour and adding these pops to your wardrobe to watch it come alive. Start small and build up..

Focal point

Always think about what the purpose of the accessory in the outfit is. Is it a function or feature? Do you simply need a handbag, in which case you probably want it to blend seamlessly with your outfit or do you want the accessory to be the feature? Think about the yellow neon shoes worn with the navy outfit I mentioned above. The feature of this look is going to be the shoes. The talking point of this outfit is going to be the shoes. Everyone will be focused on the shoes.

Body shape

Most people have an accessory type that they favour, more than others and it's usually because it flatters their shape. Whether it's scarves to disguise a full bust or tote bags that draw the eye away from the waist and balance proportions, or earrings to divert attention upwards. Using accessories as master tools of deflection; look here, not there, is a savvy way to style your outfits and will ensure you look balanced, in proportion and always on point when you leave the house.

Bags, belts and beyond

Accessories are often a very big gap in our wardrobes, often we have lots of clothes but nothing to pull those clothes together and turn them into fabulous outfits. That's where accessories come in, but where to start. What should you invest in? I think the first thing to consider is that its not simply a process of rushing out and buying loads of accessories, it's a slow process, a collection you cultivate over time, investing in pieces that you simply fall in love with and will stand the test of time as well as others that simply complement a specific outfit and those more classic, versatile pieces that you can wear across the board. The key is a mixture of each so your accessories are always strategically placed for a reason and not just there for the sake of it. Let's have a look at the main options and compare this to what you already have.

1 Necklaces: It's good to have a selection of necklaces in your collection. Long line ones are wonderful for layering over shirts and blouses to elongate proportions. Shorter chains are great for drawing the eye up and creating a statement focal point. If you already have a few necklaces of different lengths, experiment with layering them together to add texture and interest; either on top of an outfit or on the skin in an open neckline. Or layer a statement piece on top of a shirt or blouse buttoned up for gravitas.

2 Rings: A statement ring goes a long way for that little finishing touch. Something anyone, of any shape or size could adopt quite easily; it can add an extra dimension to your outfit as well as draw the eye strategically away from middle zones. Rings don't have to be expensive or solid gold; high street costume jewellery is simply perfect for this. This is the perfect accessory to add a playful element to your outfits.

3 Earrings: If necklaces don't work for you, earrings are your new best friend. A brilliant way to add that unexpected touch of personality to your look. Don't be a wallflower with your choices either, a splash of colour will add vibrancy to your outfit and a glow to your skin tone. Longer chandelier style drops will elongate a neck and add a level of sophistication to an outfit, best worn with a flat neckline so they don't compete with a collar.

4 Bracelets: Wonderful for diverting the eye from your waist to your wrist. Layered together for a more casual boho vibe, chunky for a stronger style statement and eye-catching appeal. A great alternative to necklaces and earrings if they don't work for you.

Try and put more thought into the handbag that enhances the outfit you're in.

Style Challenge 1

> Go through your jewellery and see what you've got decluttering any you don't need as you go along.

5 Belts: I'm fondly known by my team as the 'Queen of Belts' – if there was ever such a thing. To say I'm a little obsessed would be an understatement. I will add a belt onto pretty much everything and everyone. It's rare for an outfit to not look better with a belt. It needn't be a statement belt, but by adding something in the midline not only defines the waist but also draws attention to the belt and away from the tummy area. May not feel logical, but trust me it works. Try it!

There are infinite sizes and styles of belts to choose from, and there really isn't a definitive blanket rule as to what to choose, it really depends mostly on what works best with the outfit. Don't be scared or put off by the fact that you have a tummy and worry a belt will draw attention to that. A great styling trick is a high waisted trouser which nips in the waist, worn with a blouse, slightly billowed over the top of the trousers and a waisted belt with striking buckle added at the waist, below the blouse. Give this a try and watch your tummy disappear from sight.

Often a dress or jumpsuit comes with a belt in the same fabric, this is perfect for defining a waist without drawing attention to a tummy.

Experiment with tying the belt to the side, or off centre so as to draw the eye away from the midpoint of a tummy. Fabric belts can also be added to other outfits especially if a bold colour or print.

Style Challenge 2

> Try adding a belt to each outfit you wear this week. Don't worry if you wear the same belt each day, I just want you to get into the habit of adding a belt to your outfits.

6 Handbags: Most women, even the less fashion conscious among us, love a handbag or two. It's usually something that my clients have in abundance. A collection, procured over the years but sadly not used to its full potential, with the same bag thrown on day to day, no matter what the occasion. Am I right?

If you've got a wide selection of handbags, but stick to the same one most days, try and put more thought into the handbag that enhances the outfit you're in. I find keeping the contents of my handbag to a few essential items (keys, lipstick, purse, phone) means I can switch handbags more easily. Carrying a heavy handbag around is awful for posture too, so perhaps investing in a smaller tote or cross-body bag will encourage you to declutter the contents of your bag too; brilliant!

The style of handbag you wear most is often driven by practicality and in part body shape. I personally love a cross body bag as I'm less likely to lose it when it's attached to me, but if you've got a large bust, a shoulder or handheld tote will be more flattering.

Have a look at your handbag collection, large or small and see what styles and colours you have. If it is all neutral, then a pop of colour or even a metallic (silver or gold) could breathe new life into your outfits and add a much-needed zing. Try your handbag on with your outfit before you leave the house. Is it adding or detracting from your look?

7 Shoes: Like handbags, shoes are another area most women have in abundance. Once again, one style tends to dominate based on comfort and lifestyle factors, which is absolutely ok. But like handbags, could expanding the style of shoes you have in your collection add a new dimension to your outfits? If you live in trainers every day, consider swapping for other flats, sandals or boots. A small change, can totally uplevel an outfit and take it from casual to something a bit more stylised.

Many have totally stopped wearing heels since the pandemic and live in flats, but there really is nothing like a bit of a heel to improve one's proportions. The key is comfort. There is an association that heels are uncomfortable, which they absolutely can be, but there are so many options available now that are not. Choosing a block style heel is immediately better than a stiletto, ankle straps provide extra support and lots of technology has been invested into extra cushioning for comfort.

Trainers are a bit like jeans, easy to throw on with anything without having to think too much about it.

Being bolder is about putting more thought into what we wear and all the small details, like our shoes and accessories. As you're on this journey with me, my advice is to stop wearing your trainers for a week and force yourself to wear some of the other shoes in your collection, always giving thought to what shoe works best with what you're wearing. And remember, a bit of a lift, even a smallish heel, improves posture and elongates proportions. Try it and see.

Style Challenge 3

Ditch trainers for a week and force yourself to be creative with your other footwear options.

8 Scarves: A scarf is a wonderful way to inject colour, texture or print into an outfit. A long-printed scarf layered over a blazer in spring, a short neck scarf worn with a t-shirt in summer or a faux fur stole to add a touch of glamour to a blazer or coat in winter. The options are infinite and such an easy way to experiment with wearing more colour and print. If you want to disguise a bust a long scarf draped around your neck and worn long or tied loosely on the tummy, will elongate proportions perfectly. To draw attention away from hips and bum adding a neck scarf or faux fur stole will add drama and draw the eye up. The only thing to consider is the brighter the better when it comes to scarves, there is no point wearing something neutral. I am secretly hoping that by this stage, that's not something you would even consider doing. Phew!

> "Choose accessories which complement the overall style of the look you want to achieve and the overall vibe of the event you're going to."

How to accessorise

With the wide range of accessories available there is a huge choice. It's a skill to create a look, with the right number of accessories to give an outfit the wow-factor without being overcooked. Things to consider when accessorising an outfit are:

Placement

Try to space your accessories out evenly on an outfit. For instance, if you're wearing a statement necklace, don't choose large earrings as this will overcrowd the neckline. Alternatively, if you wear button or hoop earrings for a daytime look, then the accessory statement can then be worn on the arm as a bracelet or around the waist as a belt. Ensure that a statement is being made (if that's what you're going for) and that it's not lost as the outfit looks too busy. Unless of course you're taking a leaf out of Iris Apfel's book where 'More is More and Less is a Bore', but I don't think you're anywhere close to that level of adornment, yet?

Context

This may seem obvious but consider where you are wearing the outfit and what type of dress code is appropriate when choosing accessories for a look. For instance, you wouldn't wear oversized hoop earrings to a board meeting or *Manolo* heels to Glastonbury…I know…duh. Who'd do that? No one! Choose accessories which complement the overall style of the look you want to achieve and the overall vibe of the event you're going to.

Complement vs contrast

There are two ways to style your accessory, either to complement (there but not a feature), or to make a strong style statement (using the accessory to create a focal point as described above). The easiest way to do this is to choose a contrasting colour to the outfit to create a focal point in the look. But you don't always have to go for a bold colour, metallics such as silver, gold and bronze work very well and inject shine and glam to an outfit too.

As an outfit maker

This is something to try when you've honed your styling skills a bit. Perhaps you're ready now, in which case, wonderful. To do this, we start with the accessory and build the outfit around it, rather than starting with the outfit and adding the accessories to finish it off. If you have a statement accessory, perhaps a fabulous shoe or bag that you don't wear a lot as it doesn't go with as much, then this technique is a great way to use it more.

Start with the statement accessory and see what pieces you could build around it. For example, one of my favourite bags is a fuchsia pink and lemon yellow *Kate Spade* bag that was given to me as a gift for my 50th birthday by my gorgeous Style Academy students. It's a standout piece so not something I can wear with everything, which I like, as when I do wear it, it really elevates my outfit. On days when I need an extra dose of outfit inspo, I'll start with an accessory, like my *Kate Spade* bag for example. I decide whether I want to complement the bag by styling it with similar colours in my outfit or make the bag the centrepiece of my look by keeping everything else more neutral. It's a different way to build an outfit, but the result is often striking.

On one occasion I styled the bag with a fuchsia pink linen suit and yellow knit underneath. All the colours looked incredible together and the bag, although the source of inspo, toned in perfectly and wasn't the main focal point of the look, but it had inspired me to style two colours together I wouldn't have normally thought of.

I guess the moral of this story is that great accessories are a wonderful source of style stimulation, don't always settle for something classic, a few statement pieces will set your wardrobe apart.

Style Challenge 4

Experiment with styling your accessories to complement, contrast and as the main focal point of your outfits this week. You may not have all the items you need to do them all, just do what you can and have fun with it, adding any gaps to your wish-list so you can experiment later on.

BOLDER NOT OLDER

The great thing about accessories is that they have more longevity than clothes.

How many is too many?

A question I so often get asked is 'How many accessories should you have in an outfit?' I think it really depends on the outfit and whether your accessories are complementing the look or the standout feature. If you're going for a feature then keep it to one bold statement with another two blending seamlessly with the outfit. If your accessories are there to enhance but not detract then, three or four is a good starting point. For example, a floral dress could be accessorised with a belt, earrings, shoes and bag. If you're wearing a blouse and blazer with jeans, add a statement necklace, and a more classic/ neutral ring, shoes and bag. The key as always is to experiment and have fun. Don't overthink or over analyse. Remember, you are doing this for one person only and that is YOU. So don't worry about what anyone else thinks, being bold is all about being the best version of yourself, no one else.

Colour and print aside, accessories will always turn an average outfit into an amazing one, so it's definitely worth spending time this week having a play with what you already have and making a note of any gaps in your collection too.

Style Challenge 5

Make a point of adding at least three accessories (includes shoes and bags) to each outfit you wear this week. And if you want to challenge yourself further then try to not repeat any accessories for a week and see how far you get.

ANATOMY OF AN OUTFIT

Happy new week,

how are you feeling? It's been a pretty intense few weeks, hasn't it? If you need a week off, take one. You don't have to finish this process in 12 weeks. I appreciate there is a lot to take on board, so take all the time you need to refresh and embed everything you've learnt so far. It's not a race, I'll still be here when you're ready. As long as you don't forget to come back!

For those of you eager to move on, let's recap what you've achieved so far:

- **You've embraced the power of a svelte silhouette with the latest shapewear innovations.**
- **You're tweaking what you wear to show off your assets.**
- **You've decluttered your wardrobe.**
- **You're planning outfits in advance with your mini capsule wardrobe edits.**
- **You've embraced colour and print with a verve and pizazz you've never done before, and you've added the finishing touches to your outfits with accessories.**

Honey, you are already a bolder, braver, more daring and courageous person than you were when you started this process 11 weeks ago. Can you feel yourself standing taller, basking in your newfound visibility, no longer the 'older' lady at the back of the room? I see you; this process is working, and we're not even done yet. Yes, there is more.

Last week, we focused on accessories and all the wonderful options available that will enable you to add your personal flair to all the outfits you wear. This week we're going to bring all the elements of the last three chapters together; colour, print and accessories to create outfits that will make you feel like you can conquer the world in a day.

It's all very well having clothes in your wardrobe but now we're going to turn those items into show stopping outfits. This is the fun part, the part where you get to be your own personal stylist, thinking, planning and curating outfits for the week ahead.

Yes, I know you're already in the swing of styling outfits from the many challenges I've set for you throughout the book. Have you found them useful by the way? On the whole we've been focusing on individual elements in each chapter and now we're going to concentrate on pulling complete outfits together, including all these elements, accessories and all.

I've been referring to 'complete outfits' a lot throughout this book, it's how I approach my styling with clients. I never style my clients in items, and always outfits. So they walk away knowing exactly what goes with what and not having to think twice about how to style the pieces they bought together. Obviously, I can't do the same for each and every one of you, but hopefully this chapter will give you a taste of the real thing and some inspiration for when you're pulling your weekly capsule edits together.

The essential building blocks of an outfit in essence are:

- **A colour**
- **A print**
- **A neutral (see classic and interesting neutrals in Week 8)**
- **An accessory or two.**

A complete outfit should include at least two of these building blocks to create a finished look, but you'll quickly find you're including three if not all four in each outfit. Which elements you choose to include in an outfit is up to you. This is just an easy way to get your creative juices flowing and have fun with how you style your outfits. This is your chance to experiment and get creative but it also serves as a useful reference when you assess your outfit before leaving the house. Look in the mirror and ask yourself, is there something extra you could add?

Here are some combinations to illustrate how this works. I've tried to keep this as high level as possible. It's up to you to pick the specifics that are relevant to the look you're trying to achieve. Also notice, sometimes I've doubled up on an element e.g. with a colour block, this works too. You don't need to have one of each individual element in order to create a balanced look.

The options are endless, and you can adapt this formula to all aspects of your lifestyle. You can up the colour and print element in a look or tone it down with a mix of interesting neutrals and accessories. Don't feel you have to do dopamine dressing every day as long as your look is thought out and finished off with accessories. Remember it's the outfit that's all important, not the items. An individual item may not be that exciting in isolation but when styled into an outfit, it comes to life.

Two Colours and Accessories

In this outfit I've styled a colour block with the pink trousers, purple blouse and added accessories in the form of a silver belt and shoes. Not a neutral in sight.

A Print and Accessory

The print on this dress creates a natural print clash which I love and I've teamed it with red shoes as my accessory. If I was to add another layer it would probably be a black faux fur coat which would be the neutral.

Colour, Print, Neutral and Accessories

It's all going on in this look but it works. The monochrome suit (print) is centre stage and to this I've added a statement necklace, belt and black heels (accessory and neutral), and finished off with the red coat (colour). A great example of a perfectly balanced look.

Colour, Print and Accessories

Here the green trousers (colour) are centre stage so I've added a blouse (print) to complement and finished off with a colour block with the pink belt and shoes (accessories).

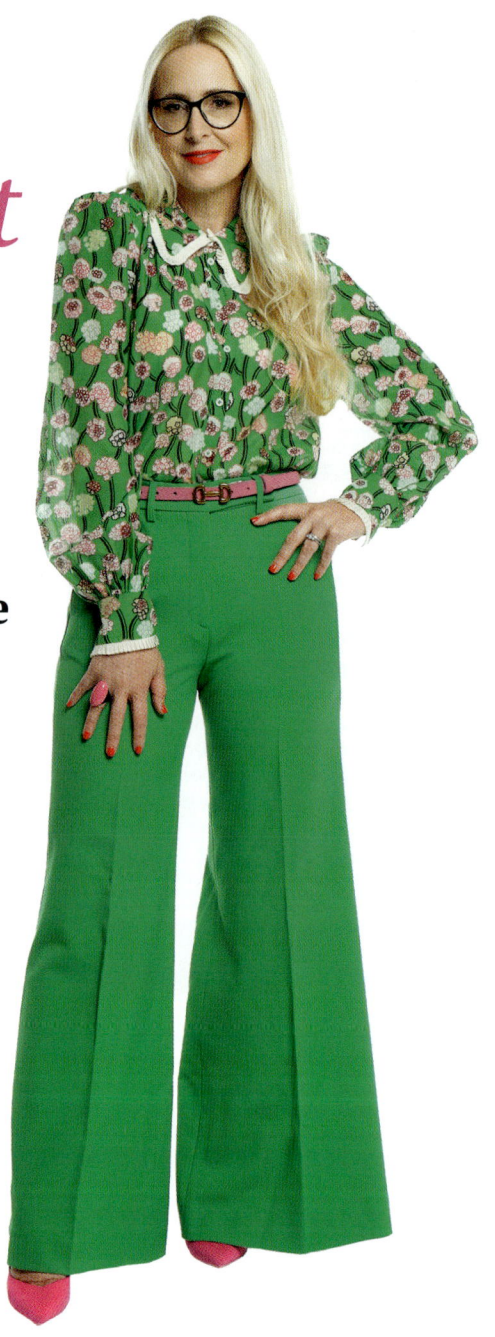

Colour, Print and Accessories

Another example of this: blouse (print), trousers (colour) and orange shoes and bag (accessories).

Colour, Print and Accessories

Playsuit (print), blazer (colour) and red heels, pink earrings and blue ring (accessories).

Two Colours, Print and Accessories

Striped trousers (print), blazer and blouse (colour block). Red shoes and blue belt (accessories).

I hope this will be a useful tool to help focus the mind and do a mental outfit check when you leave the house to ensure you have at least two elements covered and hopefully all four will soon become second nature and require minimal thought, that said, feel free to drop the 'neutral', that's absolutely not essential but sometimes a needed option to have especially if you're easing in to outfit building.

Style Challenge 1

> Ensure you have a mix of elements in each look you wear this week. Do a quick assessment in the mirror before you leave the house, to make sure you're wearing a complete outfit; add something extra if you feel it's lacking.

That's got to have been one of your easiest week's yet?! You've done all the hard grind, pushed yourself out of your comfort zone when it comes to wearing colour and print, and this week you've pulled all the building blocks of an outfit together. Is everything starting to fall into place and make sense? Hopefully by now, what to wear each day is becoming less of a stress as your photo outfit bank grows and you're getting bolder about trying new things. It's happening!!!! No turning back now.

Last but not least, did someone say shopping?!

MASTERING THE SHOPPING GAME

It's Week 12,

where did the time go? You have done so well to get this far. I hope you are feeling proud of yourself and how much you've achieved over the last 11 weeks. Even if you haven't yet managed to complete all the tasks, don't worry, there's still time, but what's most important is that you have invested time and energy to change the way you dress and most importantly the way you look and feel about yourself.

Less stress, more style

This week is a fun week, the cherry on the cake after all your hard work the past 12 weeks but how to shop well is an art.

Yes, it's something that's easily done, but so often the result is average and ends up cluttering your wardrobe. This week I'm going to share with you my top tips on how to be an expert shopper, saving yourself time and money. Yes, you heard that right, save not overspend! So many ladies will hit the shops for a fun day out with friends and come back with a load of purchases they just don't need, that don't fit properly, or only to discover that they've already got something similar in their wardrobes. We've all been there.

But we're not here to dwell on our expensive mistake buys, we're here to move forward boldly, head held high and learn how to shop like a stylist, so you only spend money on the things that you need, things that enhance your wardrobe, align with the look you're trying to achieve but most importantly bring you joy. Getting dressed every day should be a positive experience, wearing a great outfit should put a spring in your step and a smile on your face, that's what it feels like to live a bolder life. You're almost there.

But just to say, please don't feel pressured to buy anything at all. You may have discovered a whole new wardrobe out of the clothes you already have after your intensive detox and are enjoying all the fabulous outfits you've been creating from your wardrobe edit. In which case, amazing; feel free to postpone this chapter until such time as you need to buy a few key pieces to update your outfit selections.

If you do however have gaps in your wardrobe, and you can afford to do so, then shopping with purpose is most definitely the way forward. But before we dive into your shopping list, let's quickly touch on some key wardrobe essentials that may be worth considering if not already on your list.

Wardrobe essentials

These are the items I find are often missing in wardrobes, they help to pull items together and will enable you to wear more of what you have. Let's call them the cornerstones of a wardrobe, items that broadly everyone should have but the style and colour is dependent on the individual and the look they're trying to achieve.

Blazers

A good blazer instantly transforms any outfit. It's the layer, if you live in the UK, that you simply can't live without. When I say any outfit, I mean it. Literally any outfit, even sweatpants and trainers with a blazer will instantly elevate. As much as a black and a navy blazer are easy throw-ons. You can add so much style to your wardrobe with a colourful blazer or two. I collect blazers, when I see a blazer in a gorgeous colour, I buy it. I've been slowly building up my collection for years and I wear them all the time. They're probably one of the most versatile items in my wardrobe and if you're using my 'Style Formula' mixing colour and print, a coloured blazer makes it so much easier.

In terms of style of blazer, it really doesn't matter. Pick a style that works for your shape and flatters your curves. If unsure, try on a few different styles to see what suits you best. My only advice is to avoid oversized, boyfriend style blazers unless you're tall and slim. In my experience structure and tailoring in a blazer always wins.

Blouses

Button down blouses with a collar, preferably in a print, will always stand you in good stead and are often a gap in my client's wardrobe. A collar helps define a jawline, always helpful as we can lose definition in this area as we age. Unbutton to flatter a larger bust (layer over a cami if needed) or button up with a necklace for a smaller chest. I find satin blouses hugely versatile as they add an element of luxe but are cooling to wear and if they come in a print, they are extra flattering too.

Belts

You already know how much I love a belt and I hope by now you're in the habit of wearing one as often as possible. So I'm hoping you've added a few belts to your shopping list. As a general rule of thumb I would say start off with a black belt, and a metallic belt (silver or gold or both). Then add to this a leopard or animal print belt and lastly a coloured belt (any colour will do). Once you've got those nailed I guarantee you'll be hooked.

In terms of style, I would recommend trying a skinny waisted belt as a starting point. Look in particular for belts with an elasticated back or a bit of stretch as this helps to cinch in the mid-point and are often more comfortable to wear. A cheeky tip is to buy some coloured elastic in different widths and take them to a seamstress. Ask them to neaten the ends and add one or two press studs for fastening and you've got a belt! An easy and cost-effective way to expand your belt collection and add a splash of colour to an outfit.

Boots

I mentioned how we've all got a bit lazy when it comes to our footwear. A more stylish alternative to a trainer is an ankle boot, supportive, comfortable and if you can manage a bit of a heel, they will give you a much-needed lift. Ankle boots are as versatile as a trainer, but uplevel the style of an outfit a lot. When my clients present their trainer-drobe, my first question is do you have any ankle boots? No? Then it's time to get some. Remember our bold quest when purchasing though, silver or gold are as versatile and a lot more fun than black. Just saying!

Lazy jean

Most people have a lot of jeans, mostly blue, maybe black or grey if you're lucky, and usually in one style, usually skinny. Let's face it, denim is one of those items that women have in bucket loads and tend to live in them day to day, yet one of the biggest requests I get asked is how do I get out of wearing jeans all the time? The answer is it takes effort and options. Denim is such an easy throw on, it's very easy to fall into what I call the ' Lazy Jean' trap. The best way to avoid being a 'Lazy Jean' is to have other trouser or skirt options in your wardrobe to choose from, that aren't denim. Another way of elevating your denim-drobe is to experiment with different styles of jeans. If you're in a skinny rut, try a barrel or cropped flair to mix things up a bit.

> "Ankle boots: the ultimate style chameleons, taking you seamlessly from casual days to chic nights."

Shirt dresses

This is a dress style that most ladies can wear, it adds structure, flatters curves and when you find one in a bold colour or print, it will always make you look stand out and effortlessly stylish. It usually comes with a belt, often in the same fabric as the dress, which instantly helps to define the waist. My advice is to play with the belt, depending on your shape, tied in a bow to the front for a statement, or off centre to the side, or at the back to flatter a tummy. Buttoned or unbuttoned depending on your bust, it's always an all-round winner. If you don't own one, add it to your shopping list and give it a try.

The co-ord

A co-ord or suit is a great wardrobe addition. And I'm not talking about a work suit. A printed co-ord or suit in a pop of colour will add an extra dimension and versatility to your wardrobe and outfit combinations. What I love about a two-piece is that you can add it to your weekly capsule and instantly create three outfits from it. 1. As is, teamed with a t-shirt and trainers for example for the perfect laid back sophistication 2. Style the jacket/blazer with a shirt and jeans 3. Wear trousers on their own with a shirt or blouse and different blazer. Once you get started, the outfit options are usually endless. It's a value-add investment for your wardrobe.

Coats

You've probably heard this before but people can make first impressions in as little as 50 milliseconds or less and it can take as long as 7 seconds to form a complete judgement. Considering how small this window is coupled with the fact that we want to be more visible when we walk into a room and how much of the year our coat is the first thing people see; make it worthwhile looking at. Even if you're on the fence about wearing colour, my advice is start with your coat. Get the boldest, brightest one you can find and test it to see how good it makes you feel and how many people notice when you walk into a room.

The bits and bobs

I get that this is a very simplified list but that's the whole point. It's based on the areas my clients are often most lacking in their wardrobes. This is not meant to be a comprehensive list, rather areas that I believe are worth exploring and potentially adding to your wish list. Don't feel you have to add any of this to your shopping list though. I only want you to buy things that you really need. Perhaps you have enough on your shopping list already, start there and you can add on other pieces at a later date.

Style Challenge 1

Have a quick scout through your wardrobe to see which essential items from the list above are missing. Add them to your shopping-list if you want to.

Your shopping wish list

It's finally time to turn your wish list into a real life shopping list – exciting! But before you get carried away, remember the only things that should go on your shopping list are items you really need to enable you to create the looks you identified in your vision board from Week 2 so you can truly embrace your new bolder life and look.

If since your detox, your wardrobe has been somewhat decimated, don't worry, we are starting as we mean to go on, but we have to start somewhere. If your starting point is to rebuild your wardrobe from scratch, then your shopping list will inevitably be longer than someone who's rediscovered clothes and outfits in their existing wardrobe they never knew they had.

Sit down and write down items you really need in your wardrobe. Let's focus on NEED rather than WANT at this point.

What to add to your list:

- **Any items already identified as needed as you've gone through this transformation process.**

- **If you've had to throw away your favourite pair of black ankle boots as they'd seen better days and you could really do with a replacement, add them to your list.**

- **If you're missing a few pieces that would make your capsule wardrobe building a lot easier, e.g. a blue blazer, a pink camisole top, indigo straight leg jeans etc. Add them to your list.**

- **If there are a few items off your style cards that you don't have and would enable you to finish off those looks from your vision board, add them to the list.**

- **Key underwear pieces that you don't currently own e.g. shapewear pieces I referred to in Week 4, a new bra following a bra fitting or some crisp fresh briefs. Add them all too.**

- **Any items from the wardrobe essentials I mentioned above that are glaring gaps in your wardrobe; add them too but start small and build up i.e. one belt, one blazer etc.**

Only add things that are already on your wishlist, need replacing, are a gap on your vision board, a recommended must-have or a much-needed addition like underwear. Nothing else.

Now let's sort your wish list into a focused shopping list using the table as a guide. Keep the 'Brand' column clear for now, I'll go into that later.

Keep going until you've written everything on your wishlist down. The more specific and prescriptive you can be the more successful the outcome is likely to be.

Style Challenge 2

Create your shopping list.

Your shopping list is looking very exciting! Well done on clearly identifying the items you need, I am very excited to see lots of colour, print and a few accessories in there too.

List at the ready, it's time to hit the shops – woohoo.

Not so fast, we've still got some preparation to do. It's a classic mistake that so many people make, they go shopping without much of a plan or thought as to what they actually need or where they're going to find it. The result is walking into a store, feeling overwhelmed with choice and options leading to giving up and either coming home empty handed, depressed and totally frustrated or getting side-tracked and buying a load of stuff they didn't need in the first place. Sound familiar? Even if you love shopping, it's never as easy as it seems. Follow these steps to ensure shopping success. I've split these tips into in-store and online shopping to suit your preference.

> "There is no point shopping in places where the items may be fabulous, but in the most part unaffordable."

Item	Style	Colour / Print	Purpose	Brand
Blazer	Single breasted	Red	Smart / Casual	
Trousers	High waisted, slim fit	Burgundy	Work	
Blouse	Pussy bow	Animal print	Work / Going out	

In-store shopping

Where possible, I always recommend shopping in-person as much as possible as it's really useful to be able to try something on, especially if it's a brand you haven't worn before.

10 steps to successful in-store shopping

1 Set a budget
Before you buy anything, set yourself a realistic budget. There should never be any pressure to spend money on expensive clothes. Don't set yourself a budget that will put pressure on your finances. Less is more; if you have a small budget don't feel pressured to go for volume, opt instead for a few select quality pieces and build up over time. Investing in a good quality blazer for example will help you to stand tall for 10 years or more. Setting a budget will help control your spending and avoid impulse purchasing, but it also helps you identify brands that fit within your financial constraints. There is no point shopping in places where the items may be fabulous, but in the most part unaffordable. The high is always short lived and the pain of paying off expensive purchases lasts long. Set a budget before you start and stick to it.

2 Do your research
Before you hit the shops, I would suggest spending an hour online researching the items on your wish-list. For example, if you've got a red pair of high waisted, straight leg trousers on your list, go to Google and enter those terms exactly 'red high waisted straight leg trousers' and add 'womens and uk' or relevant country at the end. A list of brands and items will appear. Now click on the 'Products' tab at the top of the search results instead of 'All' and a list of images from brands with prices will appear. Go through the images and identify any brands and items that fit your requirements. The benefit of doing this is that it saves time trawling shops to find what you need, but it also exposes you to new retailers you may not have heard of or considered before.

Stock check
There's nothing more frustrating than finding something online and then it's not in-store when you get there. To avoid wasting time and energy, do a store stock check online for your size (if the option is available), or order it online for store collection. Note I mention store and not home collection, I really would prefer you to shop in person if possible. If not, then home delivery is your next best option. Write down the store next to the item on your list. It's worth researching a few options for each item in case the first option isn't suitable, so you always have a back-up plan to save time. Continue this process for each item on your list.

3 Route map
Now that you've identified a list of brands that stock the items you're looking for, it's worth researching where they are located, as ideally you want to pick a shopping location where you can access the majority within an easy walk of each of them. Shopping is tiring, so the less you need to travel between retailers the more energy you will conserve. Also consider changing room queues; start early, ideally when stores open, avoid lunchtimes. Generally, the smaller the store, the smaller the queue.

It is worth being mindful of this when planning your route to avoid wasting time standing around waiting to try on your new finds which can suck the fun out of the whole experience. The more you plan your day, the more productive you are likely to be and the less chance you have of veering off-piste.

4 Set a date
Once your route has been chosen, set a date for your shopping trip. Allocate at least half a day to shop so you don't have any time pressures. Having time pressures, results in rushed decisions and mistake buys. Make sure everyone in the family knows you aren't available during this time so you can really savour and enjoy the experience. Think of it as carving out some much needed me-time, and do not shop with a friend, or anyone for that matter unless they're a pro stylist. This is not a social endeavour, you're a girl on a mission with a comprehensive shopping list. You do not have the mental space or energy to deal with anyone else, this is all about you and your transformation.

Plan what you're going to wear ahead, so the morning is relaxed and fun. Lastly, if you have an item from your wardrobe that you want to find something to match to, it's worth packing that in advance too. Ideally don't bring too many things, as you don't want to be overloaded before you even start.

5 On the day
The day has finally arrived. Make sure you're wearing your most comfortable outfit (identified above) with pieces that are easy to take on and off. Nothing worse than wearing something you have to struggle in and out of all the time. A neutral bra and underwear is sensible too and it's also worth wearing or bringing your new contouring shapewear briefs or body, to give an outfit its best chance of looking good. Underwear lines will kill any look before it's had a chance to get off the ground.

Don't forget comfortable shoes, sore feet drain energy and lead to a negative shopping experience. A refillable water bottle and a bag of nuts or snack bar will help keep energy levels up and don't forget your lipstick, obviously being mindful of transferring it on to clothes, but a bright lipstick helps to lift a complexion and offset the draining lighting you so often get in changing rooms.

6 Arriving in store
When you arrive at your shopping destination, remind yourself of your list before entering the first store. Focus on the items you have already identified in advance. It's very easy to feel overwhelmed or get distracted by the dazzling array of new-ness at the front of the store. Retailers are very good at catching your eye as you walk in with window displays and strategically placed items at the front of the store. Be like an eagle homing in on its prey, keep focused on the task at hand. You've done your research, you know what you're looking for, go and get it. Once you've collected the items, take them straight to the changing room.

7 The changing room
We all know that changing room mirrors appear to add pounds and showcase your shape at its worst. Cellulite you didn't even realise you had (and probably don't to the naked eye), suddenly appears in bucket loads. Your frown lines seem enhanced and you look a dress size bigger than you actually are. We've all been there. I have no idea why retailers haven't cottoned on to the fact that flattering lighting sells clothes! Never mind. If you find yourself standing in a fitting room staring at yourself in your underwear, be aware of any negative messages that crop up in your head. Remember, they are not welcome here. You are bolder, brighter and soon to be more gorgeous than you've ever been, kick those negative voices into touch as your alter ego would say and focus on the outfit instead.

I recommend trying all items you've brought to the changing room, relegating anything totally awful to the discard pile instantly. Put anything good aside and once you've tried everything on once, go back and refine your choices (you have a much clearer perspective the second time around). Before finalising your selection, evaluate each piece according to the following criteria:

- **Is it on your list?**
- **Does it fit properly?**
- **Does it flatter your curves?**
- **Does it suit you?**
- **Does it align with the look you're trying to achieve?**
- **Does it make you feel good when you wear it?**
- **What can you style it with in your wardrobe?**
- **Is it within your budget?**
- **Can you return it for a full refund if you change your mind?**

If the answer is 'no' to two or more of the above, then it's not worthy of a purchase. If that means you come away with fewer items, that's fine. Remember the goal is to invest in things that add versatility and purpose to your wardrobe. Thinking about what other items in your wardrobe an item can be styled with is useful too as it means it can be instantly worn on purchase.

8 Take pictures
It is really helpful to take photos of each outfit you try on so you can see them from a totally different perspective. What you see with your own eyes is different to how an outfit can look in a photo. It's also very useful if you're undecided between two items or outfits. Pick the one that looks best in photo form as that's what everyone else will see.

9 Watch the budget
Each time you make a purchase note down how much you've spent and keep a tally on your outgoings. This will help you to stay within your spending limit. Try to keep focused and only buy items on your list. The real danger is the extra 'finds' you spotted along the way that find their way into your shopping basket. Try as best you can to avoid this as you don't want to go back to having a wardrobe full of clothes you rarely wear. Stick to the plan!

10 Unpacking your haul
When you get back from your shopping trip, put the kettle on, make yourself a well-deserved cup of tea or pour yourself a glass of wine and then put your feet up. Don't start rummaging through your purchases immediately. When you've had a good night's sleep and are well rested, set aside an hour to go through your shopping. Try everything on again to make sure the items really do look good on you and are fit for the purpose intended. If you've bought pieces to fill gaps in your wardrobe, make sure you try them on with these items in your wardrobe, to ensure they work in the way you need them too. If the outfits are a hit, remember to take photos and add them to your ever-growing outfit photo bank.

Anything that's not quite right needs to be returned as soon as possible. Hopefully this won't be the case, but if it is, book an hour in your diary to do this sooner rather than later, so they don't clutter up your newly curated, perfect wardrobe space.

There you have it. My failsafe 10 step formula to successful shopping in-store. It may seem a little laborious, but each step is pretty quick and easy. Together they are guaranteed to save time and money, minimising mistakes and frustration. Even if you're an anti-shopper, you'll be converted to this process once you've done it. And the best part is you also get to spend time with yourself.

Online shopping

In person shopping has so many benefits and should always be your first port of call, as I firmly believe we always buy less when we know we have to make another trip to return. However, if it's simply not practical for you, perhaps there are no shops nearby, you have a busy job and family life or mobility issues which preclude you from going to the shops, then online shopping is your next best option. There are also more and more brands, especially small ones, that are only available online. Here are my top tips for mindful online shopping:

7 tips for online shopping success

1 Set a budget
Just because you're shopping online doesn't mean you should do it mindlessly. Set a budget as you would for an in-store shop and stick to it, however you often need to speculate to accumulate i.e. buy more than one size to find the perfect fit. To avoid giving your credit card a beating look at alternative payment methods such as Paypal or Klarna that will allow you to pay in 30 days time, or spread the cost over 3 payments. This can massively reduce the initial outlay on your credit card and avoid unnecessary interest charges whilst you wait for refunds to come in.

2 Book a slot
Don't shop on the sofa with a glass of wine; you'll always end up with something surplus to requirements. Book out a few hours in your diary, put your phone on silent and shop with a clear head, fresh mind, focus and intention.

3 Stick to the plan
Don't get sidetracked by special offers, sale items and shiny new things. Start with the first item on your list, research it (as mentioned above) and purchase the best option. Distract yourself from all the marketing noise and only buy what you need.

The only exception to this is sizing. Approach online shopping like we'd shop in person. In the store we would take different styles, colours, and sizes to try on and then we buy the best fit. If you've never tried a brand before, it's worth buying two size options to try. Similarly, if a blouse you like comes in more than one colourway, try both, as colours in daylight are different than online. Often, it's a style or colour you least expect that looks the best.

4 The checks
Make sure you read the materials in the garment to check for allergies or fabrics that you'd prefer to avoid. Reading reviews can be helpful to gauge quality and fit. Check return and refund policies, some items are not refundable. Always make sure you are able to return items for a full refund before purchasing

5 **The sale**
Once done, save confirmation emails in a folder for reference in case you need to return an item. Make a list of all your purchases, how much you've spent on each item and where you got the items from for reference, so you can keep track of deliveries. It also helps when deciding between items to keep or return if the budget is limited.

6 **The arrival**
As your purchases start to arrive, wait until everything has been delivered before diving in. Then do exactly as I recommend in point 10 above: 'Unpacking your haul'. Block out some time to try everything on without distraction. Any items or sizes that don't work, should be repackaged, and labelled for postage as quickly as possible. All items that pass the test should be styled into outfits; photos taken and integrated into the right place in your wardrobe, so as not to upset the beautifully organised status quo.

7 **Managing returns**
Make a list of the items you need to return and tick them off as you action each. Check return refund policies so you don't miss out and make a note next to each brand item. Missed return dates are one of the biggest culprits of mistake buys cluttering up our closets.

Then make a list of refunds you are waiting for and again, tick them off as they arrive. It's not uncommon for a refund to slip through the returns net and not be actioned. Make sure you keep all postage receipts and follow up on any missing refunds that haven't been credited within 21 days. Online shopping can be an admin headache, you must be on it to ensure you don't lose out.

Style Challenge 3

Go shopping, in-person or online. Caveated by, only if you need to. As mentioned above I would recommend you start in-store and move to online for any extra items if required.

Phew, who knew shopping was such a technical business. Life was so much simpler when you only had one shop to choose from, but let's face it, it's a lot more fun when you have more options. It also means carving out your individuality, making bolder fashion choices and striving to always be fabulous is a whole lot easier.

And that brings us nicely to the end of Week 12 and the end of this transformation journey, sniff. Turn over for a final word before you open your new bold wings and fly.

A BOLD INVITATION

Oh my goodness,

that was a total whirlwind. I've thrown everything at you these past 12 weeks and you have taken it, embraced it and turned it into a positive force. Can I just say, how blown away I am by how far you've come on this journey especially if we consider where you were when we started off. Amazing!

CONCLUSION

You look different, feel different and there is NO going back to where you were, when you started. You've flicked that switch in your head, decluttered the frump from your wardrobe, embraced colour and print, accessorised and reinvented your outfits. This is your official invitation to step into boldness.

You are officially:

B
Brave: You take risks with your outfits.

O
Open: To new ideas, no longer stuck in your old ways.

L
Loud: Proud to be visible again, noticed, seen. No more hiding away.

D
Daring: You no longer care what other people think; in fact, you dare to be different.

E
Expressive: You've found a style that expresses who you are without having to speak.

R
Resolute: There is no turning back to where you were. This is how you roll from now on.

Yes! I love it! No wallflowers welcome in your new world. Ava would be so proud.

Remember, to look good is a lifetime commitment. It's not for a season, only to be lost and forgotten once the stress of life takes over. You start small and slowly build a wardrobe you can rely on for every occasion, which you can subtly adapt and add to over the years as your style evolves.

As you move forward, remember that this journey is ongoing. Being bold is about continually pushing your boundaries, trying new things and embracing the confidence that comes from truly being yourself. Each day offers a new opportunity to express your boldness, to refine your style, and to inspire others to do the same.

Your transformation is not just about clothes or appearance; it's a mindset. It's about waking up every day with the determination to be the best version of yourself; to live with passion and authenticity.

You've proven that change is possible at any stage of life, and now it's up to you to keep that momentum going. If I have helped you to look and feel bolder and live a brighter life, then my purpose is done.

Stay brave, open, loud, daring, expressive and resolute. Continue to challenge yourself and embrace the vibrant, fearless person you've become. Celebrate your journey and look forward to the many adventures that lie ahead. Most importantly, always be kind to yourself because you're amazing.

Transformation equals liberation, not letting age define who you are and how you look. It's time for you to become the inspiration the world needs to see.

And remember, there are no fashion police. The only rule in life you need to stick to is the speed limit in a built-up area as the consequences could be fatal. You can't kill anyone with a bad outfit, so stop worrying about what other people think because quite frankly, who cares? Trust me when I say, no one ever cares as much as you.

At the end of the day, it's your personality and your outfit, not anyone else's.

Thank you for joining me on this journey over the past 12 weeks; it's been a privilege to watch your confidence soar and your style evolve. Keep up all the hard work you've put in so far and you'll never feel average or unseen again.

Before I go, I was reminded of this wonderful poem by Jenny Joseph which so perfectly sums up why it's so important to start living a Bolder life now and not wait until you're really OLD…..

An extract from 'Warning'

By Jenny Joseph

When I am an old woman I shall wear purple

With a red hat which doesn't go, and doesn't suit me.

And I shall spend my pension on brandy and summer gloves

And satin sandals, and say we've no money for butter.

I shall sit down on the pavement when I'm tired

And gobble up samples in shops and press alarm bells

And run my stick along the public railings

And make up for the sobriety of my youth.

I shall go out in my slippers in the rain

And pick flowers in other people's gardens.

But maybe I ought to practise a little now?

So people who know me are not too shocked and surprised

When suddenly I am old, and start

to wear purple.

All that's left for me to say is….
Welcome to your new, bolder life!

Nicky x

CONCLUSION

I'd love to stay in touch.

CONCLUSION

Please follow me for more style tips on Instagram and TikTok

**@nickyhambletonjones
#boldernotolder**

And sign up to my newsletter at

www.nickyhambletonjones.com

Wish List

CONCLUSION

Shopping List

CONCLUSION

Acknowledgements

This book has been a labour of love, and as with any passion project, it takes a team to transform an idea into reality. I am deeply grateful to Suzi Wooldridge and Carolyn Andrews at Synergy for believing in me and giving me the opportunity to write the book I've always dreamed of creating. To Cameron Toman and the wider Synergy team, thank you for turning my words into a visual masterpiece and juggling all the many moving parts.

A heartfelt thank you to my dear friends Andrew Barton, who first introduced me to the Synergy team and to Kate Battrick for her invaluable feedback on the first draft and her guidance in shaping the overall structure of the book.

Nicole Howes, my fabulous and endlessly patient editor, deserves special mention for being a voice of calm and reason at the end of many long writing days. A huge thank you as well to Katie Read and the incredible team at ReadMaxwell for their expert help in generating exceptional publicity for this book.

Lastly, to my wonderful family: thank you for enduring the emotional roller coaster that comes with writing a book. Your love and support have meant the world to me.